CLINICIAN'S GUIDE TO TREATING

Stress After War

CLINICIAN'S GUIDE TO TREATING

Stress After War

EDUCATION AND COPING
INTERVENTIONS FOR VETERANS

JULIA M. WHEALIN, PhD • LORIE T. DECARVALHO, PhD • EDWARD M. VEGA, PhD

WILEY

John Wiley & Sons, Inc.

We dedicate this manual to the men and women who bear the weight of battle in their lives. There is no way to thank you enough for your remarkable courage, strength, and sacrifice in serving our country.
We also appreciate the efforts of all of the active duty and civilian clinicians devoted to working with veterans and their family members. Thank you for your committed support of our war veterans.

Contents

Preface

Left untreated, war-related stress can lead to a number of negative outcomes ranging from poor concentration, hypervigilance and chronic anger, to domestic violence, substance abuse, incarceration (e.g., Saxon, Davis, Sloan, McKnight, McFall, & Kivlahan, 2001) and mortality (e.g., Drescher, Rosen, Burling, & Foy, 2003). However, it is possible for veterans to understand, learn to cope with, and experience relief from their symptoms, resulting in a better quality of life.

Researchers over the past twenty years have concluded that early intervention for war-related stress can prevent or lessen the likelihood that PTSD and other losses will occur (e.g., Foa, Keane, & Friedman, 2000; Litz, 2004). Psychoeducational interventions promote resilience to the impact of traumatic stress (e.g., Raphael & Wooding, 2004). These include interventions that educate veterans about common acute or posttraumatic stress reactions and provide coping skills. Treatment Guidelines from the Veteran Affairs, the Department of Defense, and major organizations such as the International Society of Traumatic Stress Studies recommend psychoeducation as a first line intervention for acute and posttraumatic stress disorders (Foa, Keane, & Friedman, 2000).

We developed the present intervention for veterans who are identified as at-risk for PTSD and related disorders. Rather than taking a pathogenic perspective, however, this treatment program emphasizes a wellness model. Further, we address these issues from an empirical background, accepting the reality that highly stressful events such as combat experiences result in numerous common reactions and symptoms. The focus of this program is to help individuals:

- Understand the reactions they are experiencing
- Become better able to negotiate common problems associated with combat stress that negatively impact day-to-day life
- Practice behaviors that increase resilience and facilitate the healing process

All of the information we present in this manual and in the accompanying workbook (*Strategies for Managing Stress After War: Veteran's Workbook and Guide to Wellness*) is derived from empirically-validated treatment methods, cognitive behavioral theory, the latest scientific research on psychological resilience, and best practice guidelines for acute and traumatic stress. Additionally, the information is further augmented by direct assessment of returnee needs, our experiences consulting and collaborating with military and VA professionals, and over twenty years in combined experience providing clinical interventions for veterans suffering from combat stress reactions.

This treatment program may be used by clinicians working with veterans in individual or as a group therapy approach. It consists of an eight-section psychoeducational treatment program. The eight chapters address key areas that are of particular concern to veterans. In each chapter, we focus on teaching information and skills that promote better health and better outcomes. These key areas are:

- Increasing understanding of normal combat stress reactions
- Improving stress management and coping skills
- Sleep hygiene
- Management of anger/irritability
- Skillfully negotiating interpersonal problems
- Assimilating back into society and family life

This program is intended as a first line intervention for those suffering from combat stress. However, clinicians using this manual should not limit themselves to these techniques, as there are a number of other effective complementary interventions, such as Exposure Therapy (Foa, Hembree, & Rothbaum, 2007) and Cognitive Processing Therapy for PTSD (Resick & Schnicke, 1993). Importantly, additional interventions will be necessary for veterans at risk for harm, or who are suffering from major disorders or severe traumatic grief.

Through the use of this manual, we hope to help you, the clinician, work to promote health and healing among those who have served in our nation's armed services. Our goal is to provide for you:

- Tools for personal and individualized self-assessment of symptoms and concerns before, during, and after the intervention
- Practical suggestions, tips, skills, techniques, and questions to enable veterans to work at their own pace on the unique problems they may be experiencing
- Practical handouts, worksheets, and quizzes that may be used before, during, and after this program to ensure continued healing and growth for veterans

Our nation's combat veterans have made extraordinary sacrifices on our behalf. Many continue to struggle with ongoing effects of combat stress; many continue to bear the cost of war. With proper treatment, veterans can begin to experience relief and healing. Through the inner strength they possess, they can begin to transform their combat experience and get on with their lives.

We would also like to take the opportunity to thank and acknowledge the clinicians who serve our nation's war heroes. Your work with our veterans is invaluable and deserving of further recognition. Thank you for your dedication and service to our veterans. It is truly an honor for us to work with you in serving those who have served.

Acknowledgments

We would like to acknowledge the contribution of the many returning warriors with whom we have spoken over the last five years as we developed and refined this treatment guide. The openness of these veterans was a key factor in helping us understand the problems faced by those experiencing combat stress. We are grateful for their willingness to share, during clinical assessments and interventions, the challenges they faced and, in most cases, overcame. We remember each of them with great warmth, appreciation, and admiration.

We also want to recognize the clinician researchers who developed the theories and interventions that helped lay the ground work for the present program. Without their dedication to advancing effective psychosocial treatments, we would not have been able to formulate this program.

Thanks to Dawn Tomita and Roxanna Montoya-Shaffer for making some of our edits to portions of this guide.

Last, we would like to acknowledge the help of those clinicians who tested this intervention protocol with various groups of veterans across the country, including Ltc. Richard Schobitz and Cot. Michael Faran of Schofield Barracks Soldier and Family Assistance Center, Dr. Miles McFall of the Seattle VA, Kelly Takasawa, and Dr. Mary Tramatin of the Bronx VA. The feedback and assessment data that you and the veterans with whom you worked helped us to evaluate and fine-tune this treatment guide.

Introduction

FOR THE CLINICIAN

Individuals who are deployed to a war zone and endure daily stressors associated with it will be profoundly affected by their experience. For some individuals, the physical, psychological, and social demands of being in a war zone are considerable. It is essential that clinicians recognize the potential impact of such stressors on returnees. Provision of early interventions, like this treatment program, may diminish the possibility of veterans developing chronic negative outcomes and lessen the functional impact of negative sequelae—such as Posttraumatic Stress Disorder (PTSD).

It is important to be cognizant of how labeling an individual with PTSD may result in stigmatization and further mental harm (Litz, 2004). For these reasons, the Stress After War program utilizes a positive treatment approach with veterans who are experiencing some symptoms of PTSD—but who do not meet full criteria—as well as for recent veterans with acute PTSD. Fully comprehending the scope of issues facing war returnees, such as the toll of reintegrating into everyday society after being in a war zone, is very important for those working with veterans. Furthermore, it is essential that we appreciate the strengths that enabled veterans to adapt to and survive the war zone environment, and to help them use their inherent coping abilities to overcome stress after war.

▶ Leader prerequisites

The Stress After War manual is geared for mental or behavioral health clinicians who have at minimum a post-graduate level of training in counseling or psychotherapy. We recommend this level of knowledge base, skills, or training so that clinicians are able to appropriately assess the needs of each veteran they are treating. Clinicians should be competent in assessing when veterans require more in-depth treatment, particularly if they show signs of being homicidal or suicidal, or if more serious psychopathology becomes evident. Additionally, clinicians using this treatment should have the training in cognitive behavior theory and methods necessary to provide both didactic interventions and instruction regarding psychotherapeutic skills—such as behavior modification, cognitive modification, arousal reduction, and stress management.

▶ Participant prerequisites

The Stress After War intervention is designed for veterans who are experiencing war-related stress reactions. Veterans should be capable of engaging with the clinician in one-on-one therapy. As previously mentioned, this treatment program may also be used as a group therapy approach with veterans. In an individual or group therapy setting, veterans who are participating should meet the following prerequisites:

- Be able to follow therapeutic rules (if applicable, group rules),
- Have at least a sixth grade reading level or overall level of comprehension,
- Possess the minimal capacity to pay attention during a one- to two-hour didactic presentation and discussion,
- Be able to maintain a contract for safety with the clinician (or group leader, as well as the group members, if applicable),
- Be clean and sober, and
- In group interventions, be courteous and respectful of others in the group.

When veterans are able and willing to contract for appropriate behaviors ahead of time, this tends to ward off later problems.

We do not recommend the Stress After War intervention for the following individuals unless a qualified professional is also treating them for those conditions:

- Veterans at mild to moderate risk for harming themselves;
- Veterans at mild to moderate risk for harming someone else;
- Veterans suffering from mild to moderate levels of Depression, PTSD, Bereavement, or other mental health disorders; or
- Veterans with active or recent substance abuse diagnosis.

Furthermore, we do not recommend the Stress After War intervention for the following specific groups of individuals because there is no evidence that this intervention will be effective for such individuals. This includes veterans who are:

- At high risk for harming themselves;
- At high risk for harming someone else;
- Suffering from severe levels of Depression, PTSD, Bereavement, or showing symptoms of psychosis (such as hallucinations, delusions, or disorganized behavior); or
- Cognitively impaired.

▶ For veterans who need more comprehensive care

Veterans who experience traumatic stress go through a normal transitional period, which may be marked by a range of problems such as insomnia and irritability. Other veterans will need additional professional referrals for more severe problems—such as violence, suicidality, and substance abuse. This intervention is not appropriate for everyone, particularly individuals who may be suffering from major psychiatric disorders and are not being treated for those conditions. If a veteran has coexisting severe or destabilizing mental conditions—such as psychosis—they are unlikely to benefit from this group until they are stabilized and followed by a mental health professional who is able to treat them.

■ Who is qualified to provide comprehensive mental health care?

Professionals qualified to provide comprehensive mental health care will usually have a doctoral level degree (M.D., Ph.D., Psy.D.) or at least a master's degree (M.S., L.C.S.W., C.S.W., M.A.) in a mental health care field. Those professionals who also have additional special training in PTSD will be able to provide more advanced treatment for trauma memories, nightmares, and bereavement. You or someone else in your clinic may have these credentials and training. If this is not the case, see the sections below and the resource section of this manual for recommendations about where and when to get help.

■ When to make a referral: Risk for harm

When the veteran presents to the clinic with combat stress symptoms, it is important during that first visit to assess him or her for dangerousness to oneself or others. If the veteran says that he or she is thinking about harming him or herself or others, it will be important to immediately assess the veteran's environment for ongoing threats and protect him or her or others from harm. Additionally, you should take immediate steps to stabilize them even if you have to refer them to another professional.

- If your client is currently in a crisis, or you are worried that he or she might hurt or kill him or herself or someone else, you should get help immediately. Take the person's concerns or threats seriously.
- If your client has plans to harm someone else, follow legal mandates based upon military procedures (if Active Duty) or the laws of your state.
- If your client has a plan to commit suicide—and you do not have the credentials to respond to such an emergency—you should get help immediately from the local hospital emergency room, 911, your military's mental health center (if Active Duty), or the Veteran Affairs 24-hour crisis line (if being treated as a veteran).

When assessing for suicide, here are some helpful questions to determine a client's level of risk. A positive response to any of these questions will indicate cumulatively higher risk for suicide:

- Does the client have a plan (for how to commit suicide)?
- Do they have the means to carry it out?
- Have they attempted suicide in the past?
- Are they alone and/or without a supportive person or persons to contact?
- Do they have a mental or physical illness or are they abusing substances?
- Have they suffered a significant recent loss?

Further, there are also emergency telephone hotline numbers that may be useful:

- National Suicide Hotline: 1-800-SUICIDE (1-800-784-2433)
- National Suicide Prevention Lifeline: 1-800-273-TALK

If violence or abuse is a problem:

- National Domestic Violence/Child Abuse/Sexual Abuse: 1-800-799-SAFE
- National Center for Victims of Crime's toll-free information and referral service: 1-800-FYI-CALL.

■ When to make a referral: Major depression, bereavement, PTSD, and other major disorders

A portion of those who present to you with interest in joining the group may also be suffering from Major Depression, PTSD, Bereavement, or other mental health disorders. Such individuals may be appropriate for this group, but should also be being treated for those conditions by a qualified professional.

Veterans who screen positive for PTSD or other mental health disorders should be provided psychoeducation, acute symptom management, and (as necessary) social and spiritual support. Additionally, these clients should be seen by a mental health clinician with advanced training for full assessment. For veterans suffering from PTSD, effective advanced treatment will consist of stabilization, education, and the development of a collaborative treatment plan, and can often involve multiple professionals.

Grief is a normal and natural response to loss but is a neglected process that can impact veterans. The diagnosis of Bereavement is used when grief warrants clinical attention. Because responding to losses and death is often awkward and uncomfortable, veterans suffering from Bereavement often avoid dealing with their thoughts and feelings related to loss. If a client is having high levels of guilt or anger about actions taken or not taken related to loss—or feel as though they should have died during the loss event—more comprehensive care may be needed. If feelings of loss are not appeased by normal social routes (such as through consulting with their chaplain), veterans should be referred to a mental health professional for full assessment and treatment. Finally, if your client's combat stress symptoms are not improved by the end of the treatment, we recommend that you refer the person for more comprehensive treatment.

▶ About the model used in this guide

The psychoeducational treatment model is designed to be applicable to both individual and group treatment contexts. There is a strong didactic emphasis to psychoeducational treatment models, which set them apart from other types of individual therapy or therapy groups. As indicated at the beginning of this chapter, we designed this treatment program to be flexible enough to be utilized with various military and veteran populations. It can be used in a one-on-one or group therapy context.

Additionally, the Stress After War treatment approach itself is designed to be maximally flexible. As such, each session can last from one to two or more hours, depending on the needs of the individual or group and time restrictions. With an average client population with a 12th grade reading level, this intervention can be administered in eight sessions lasting one and a half hours. However, it is also flexible enough to be used for shorter or longer treatment models as needed. For example, these materials would also be suitable for a 16-session group—allowing for additional time both to address the relevant information in session and for veterans to practice using the included assignments and exercises. Similarly, some individuals may benefit from additional time focused on applying skills learned in the program to particular situations or problems they may experience. Thus, the exact length of the course can vary according to the needs of the veterans, while maintaining a focus on the specific concepts and skills taught in this program.

Finally, the Stress After War intervention focuses strongly on empowering veterans to develop greater *coping self-efficacy*. Coping self-efficacy refers to the degree to which an individual feels able to tolerate and cope with symptoms. Oftentimes, veterans do not comprehend their own role in controlling their combat stress symptoms. When individuals take direct action to cope with their stress reactions and trauma-related problems they start to feel empowered. Part of the role of the clinician is instilling hope and enthusiasm so that veterans increase their sense of control over their lives. For example, we encourage clinicians to tell veterans: "This program has a lot to offer you, but it will only be effective if you actually practice the skills and apply the principles to make changes in your life." Again, our emphasis is on reinforcing the veterans' inherent abilities to take control of their lives.

▶ How to conduct psychoeducational treatment

The first basic component of conducting a psychoeducational treatment program involves providing a rationale. It is the clinicians' role to help veterans understand *what* they will gain from this treatment program and *how* they will accomplish those gains. A well planned rationale provides the initial structure to help veterans believe that they will learn how to manage their behavior, thereby impacting their coping ability and, ultimately, their symptoms.

Another basic component of conducting a psychoeducational treatment program is encouraging individuals to be actively involved in the program. Asking veterans questions during the intervention, asking them to read, and asking them to share examples from their own lives will help them better learn and incorporate the material. Similarly, it is important to occasionally check in with the veterans about their level of understanding. Even though psychoeducational treatment programs involve more a didactic presentation than more process-oriented treatments do, maintaining a flow of dialogue in the treatment enhances one's interest in and ability to understand the material.

On a related note, it is important that both the clinician and the veteran understand the goals of the intervention—and that topics do not stray to other areas. When conducting both individual and group psychoeducational treatments, it is important to guide discussion and not get lost in tangential discussions. When questions or comments distract from the session topics, we suggest that clinicians defer the question to discussion after the session is over (in the case of group treatment) or make careful decisions about the amount of time allotted to the other topics (in the case of individual treatment). Additional information regarding the theoretical background for this treatment program can be found in the Treatment Model and Theories section.

■ A note about group intervention skills

We would like to take a few moments to further discuss how to use this program in a group therapy setting. In a group context, the clinician should first screen all veteran clients to ensure that they can benefit from this treatment model. Then, there are a number of significant skills that should be utilized while conducting this program.

As part of the pretreatment screening process, clinicians should determine whether or not there are any veterans who may need more intensive psychotherapeutic intervention to address their needs. For more information about when to make an appropriate referral, please read the section in this chapter labeled when to make an appropriate referral. Group leaders should exercise the following interventions in running this group.

Determine the type of group

You will need to decide whether or not the group will be an open or closed group. An open group allows for new members to start the group at different points, while a closed group does not allow for others to come into the group after it has started. Typically, groups are closed in nature because this helps to prevent disruption or the need for group members to build rapport with new people time and again—as well as assuring that participants are able to benefit from the progression of skills being practiced in the program. However, open groups may be necessary to meet the needs of new clients who present to you for help. If appropriate, veterans can be included in deciding whether the group should be open or closed.

Set the length and duration of the group

It is important to be clear and realistic about the number of sessions and duration of the group (see also the earlier section titled "About the model used in this manual"). It is preferable to begin the group by being explicit about the number of sessions and the length. In general, do not change the timeline as this can create confusion in group members. Keep in mind that if you terminate the group sooner, group members may feel rejected or abandoned. If you terminate later than agreed upon, this can create dependency and confusion of boundaries.

Set and discuss rules with the group

Usually, group rule setting involves coming to an agreement with group members about the need for confidentiality within the group (recognizing that the therapist may also have limits to confidentiality, for example, in the case of evidence of imminent harm to a client or third party). Therefore, in the first session, we recommend asking each group member to agree that they will maintain confidentiality. We also recommend reminding group members after each session that whatever someone says in group, stays in group.

Other issues include: how to handle absences (for example, some leaders require that group members need to call beforehand to let them know that they will be absent); payment and money issues; the need to be clean and sober; the need to be respectful of others; and that no violence or threats are allowed. You should work with each specific group during the first session so that each member is clear about and agrees to follow group rules. Another important rule is that there are no cliques between group members—as this can create animosity, destroy trust, and alienate other group members. Essentially, all of these rules will enable a feeling of interpersonal safety between members of the group and facilitate healthy progress.

Negotiate group dynamics

Similar to deciding if the group is open or closed in structure, you will need to work with the group to determine how to handle communication between and among group members. You may wish to set a "no cross talk" rule as a way of handling different negative dynamics that arise. For example, you may tell group members that they need to let one person speak until he or she is finished, then they need to wait until you—as the group leader—call on them to comment. At times, group members may disagree about different issues. This is natural when you have a number of people in one room. However—as the leader—you can help negotiate conflict by making it clear that people can disagree, and that the group is not a forum for people to express or promote their individual opinions. Rather, group members need to respect other's rights to their own opinions.

Another issue that usually needs to be negotiated in the group is expectations for participation. As leader, you should decide ahead of time the appropriate degree to which veterans will be expected to participate. What happens, for example, if someone takes up a lot of time or does not let others participate or both, or if someone is very nonparticipatory. In general, we recommend that everyone have a chance to participate in each group, even if just by reading or providing an example from their lives. You can work with your group to come up with rules about this as well. Last, some individuals may have a tendency to play junior therapist—that is, one who tries to analyze or give advice to others in the group. It is good practice to discourage inappropriate advice-giving behavior as it erodes trust and can create an atmosphere of tension or resentment in other group members. When this happens, you can gently confront that individual by pointing out their behavior and reminding them of the group rules.

Decide how to handle termination of the group

Carefully consider with the group how termination will be handled. An important issue we discussed earlier was the need to clearly state how long the group will run and when it will terminate. It is good practice to begin helping group members process their feelings about termination a few weeks prior to the end date. Also, a few weeks early decide—with group members—how the last session will be handled. For example, some groups find it therapeutic to exchange notes or communicate with one another, stating what they might admire about, have learned from, or wish for each other. Other groups find it helpful to throw a farewell party. Others may wish to just say their goodbyes in a simpler and less complicated manner. Some group members may wish to carry on friendships with individuals after the group has finished and so may wish to have an exchange of contact information. In this program, this forming of connections with other group members is encouraged (e.g., through the use of the telephone calling exercise described at the end of Chapter 1), and it is common for participants in a group to remain in contact with each other following their group experience together.

For the purposes of this book, it is assumed that clinicians have an appropriate level of training, expertise, and experience in administering individual and group therapies. For more in-depth information about the application of group intervention skills with trauma, you can refer to additional resources about conducting groups located at the end of each chapter heading.

HOW TO USE THIS GUIDE

This secondary prevention intervention is a compilation of several cognitive-behavioral interventions and, as such, draws predominantly from cognitive-behavioral theory. Core components of this intervention consist of training veterans in: (a) behavioral modification techniques, such as engaging in pleasant events, challenging the tendency towards avoidance, and sleep hygiene; (b) cognitive modification techniques, such as increasing problem-solving skills; and (c) arousal reduction techniques, such as relaxation training and diaphragmatic breathing. In general, we center our treatment program upon a three-stage approach of education, acquisition of skills, and application.

This psychoeducational treatment model is divided into eight psychoeducational modules on coping with combat-related transition stress. Specific areas targeted for intervention include: (a) understanding transition stress reactions, (b) stress management, (c) healthy coping, (d) sleep problems, (e) anger, (f) reintegration into society, (g) reintegration into family, and (h) post-combat growth.

▶ Format of the guide

When using this guide there are various sections that help maximize ease of use included in each chapter. Sections within each chapter are consistent throughout the book for ease of reading and being able to locate information. We highly recommend initially reading the chapter from the beginning to the end—rather than skipping around. After you have read through the book at least once, you may be able to jump around between sections and locate particular information specific to the needs of the veteran with whom you are working.

■ Chapter outlines

Outlines for each chapter are provided in Appendix B. Each outline is designed to provide a single-page (double-sided) reminder of key points within the chapter, for use by the clinician. When first utilizing this treatment guide, it will be important for clinicians to refer to the guide frequently. However, after utilizing this treatment model several times and becoming very familiar with the material within each section, a seasoned clinician may find it useful simply to refer to the outline when conducting treatment.

■ Section title

The names of sections are consistent across the clinicians' guide and the veterans' workbook, and have the same letter designations to facilitate ease in referring to specific content. To permit matching sections to have the same title designation across the two books, sections in the guide that do not occur in the workbook (e.g., homework review) are not marked with a letter.

INSTRUCTION TO CLINICIANS

The chapters in this clinicians' guide provide comprehensive instructions for each section. Look to the sidebars within each chapter for detailed instructions to clinicians. *Sample dialogue is also provided in italics within each section.* Please note that instruction to the clinicians is unique to the guide and will not be found in the veteran's workbook.

■ When to talk to your doctor

This treatment model is designed to maximally benefit numerous common reactions to combat-related stress. These reactions are frequently very painful to experience and may interfere with normal functioning. In most individuals, these reactions are manageable and lessen over time. In some cases, however, the reactions persist or are of sufficient severity to warrant additional intervention. Clinicians should be alert to indicators of higher levels of distress, so as to provide or make referrals for additional treatment.

Near the end of each chapter, we provide a few screening questions (related to each chapter) regarding key indicators that may reflect the need for additional intervention. These sections should serve as reminders to assess regularly for high levels of distress and other symptoms that suggest veterans may need additional help.

■ Homework/On your own

Homework assignments are provided at the end of each chapter. Because this is a skills-focused treatment approach, *practicing skills consistently is critical to changing behavior and improving overall coping.* We suggest reviewing the previous homework assignment with veterans at the beginning of each session and reinforcing efforts toward successful completion of the assignment. Especially in the earlier sessions of the program, it is important to review homework in detail—both to emphasize the importance of practicing the skills they learn and to encourage veterans as they continue to make positive changes in their lives.

If the veteran has not completed a homework assignment, you may choose to focus—in an encouraging and nonjudgmental way—on factors that interfered with practice, as well as emphasizing the importance of practice. Additionally, clinicians should continue to encourage practice of earlier skills throughout the program, so that skill building and practice are cumulative. For example, although veterans will learn relaxation training in Chapter One, those skills should be practiced during the subsequent chapters,—such as when focusing on managing anger.

■ Quizzes

All eight chapters have a short quiz at the end that evaluates content knowledge. Quizzes are fairly easy and are designed to reward the veteran for his or her learning. Clinicians are able to implement quizzes according to veterans' needs. For instance, veterans may fill them out at the end of the session on their own and hand them in. If you choose this format, it can be very helpful to review the answers to the quizzes during the beginning of the following session, which serves as a review. Alternatively, the quiz can be reviewed during the same session, to provide immediate reinforcement of the material learned. If time is an issue, veterans may fill quizzes out at home. Answers to quizzes are in the Appendices of both this *Clinician's Guide* and the *Veteran's Workbook*. The answer key in the clinician's manual also includes other details useful in discussing the topics covered. To best reinforce their learning of the material, veterans should be encouraged to complete the quizzes provided at the end of each chapter prior to checking their answers.

■ Pre and post tests

We have designed surveys for clinicians, and have included them in the guide (see Appendix C) to help measure clients' progress over the course of this program. Surveys evaluate three area: Skills, knowledge, and symptoms. The Coping Skill Inventory (CSI) is a survey of the types and frequency of coping skills that veterans use. The responses are tallied for skills specific to depression, anger management, stress management, and sleep hygiene. The Coping Knowledge Inventory (CKI) measures knowledge about the material presented in the workbook and clinicians' manual. Last, a copy of a screening measure for PTSD symptoms is provided, the Primary Care PTSD Screen (PC-PTSD; Prins et al., 2004). We recommend administering, at minimum, these surveys to veterans before and after the intervention.

▶ The veteran's workbook

In addition to this manual, we developed a companion workbook—*Strategies for Managing Stress After War: The Veteran's Workbook and Guide to Wellness*. The workbook is designed to be used hand-in-hand with the clinician guide. Like this guide, the workbook can be used in a variety of ways. It can be used in a one-on-one or group therapy format, as a teaching tool for veterans and family members, or used separate from the *Clinician's Guide* as a self-help book for veterans.

The workbook is written at a sixth to eighth-grade level. Space is provided at various points in the workbook for veterans to write in answers to questions. Additionally, On Your Own sections at the end of each chapter provide after-session homework activities to help veterans implement new skills. As mentioned previously, we strongly encourage clinicians to require veterans to perform homework in between sessions. The intervention will only be effective if veterans are willing to make changes in their own lives.

TREATMENT MODEL AND THEORIES

The approaches utilized in this book are primarily informed by cognitive behavioral therapies, and incorporate a range of strategies designed to help returnees efficiently use numerous internal and external resources as they readapt to life back in the world and away from the combat theatre. Broadly speaking, cognitive and behavior therapies are active, directive, structured therapies focused on helping individuals to make specific changes in how they are thinking about things and what they are doing. Veterans are provided with specific ways to practice implementing changes that promote healing and recovery. In the following sections, we describe such related theories that inform our treatment model for returnees.

▶ Classical and operant conditioning theories

Through a process of classical conditioning, during highly stressful events many cues become associated with danger or threat. These cues then serve as reminders of the event and become able to trigger anxiety and fear reactions in the person. After such conditioning, the person may experience anxiety in many situations even though no actual threat exists. For example, trash such as discarded cola cans have been used both to build and disguise improvised explosive devises (IEDs). Operation Iraqi Freedom (OIF) and Operation Enduring Freedom (OEF) veterans who participated in convoys learned—through classical conditioning—to associate trash on the side of the road with explosions or threat of explosions. Such veterans may experience extreme distress when they see trash of similar appearance once back in the United States and begin to avoid driving. Similarly, individuals may begin to avoid other situations, thoughts, feelings, people, and other things that serve as cues for highly stressful events. Initially, avoidance may reduce anxiety—that is, through a process of operant conditioning the avoidance is negatively reinforced. However, over time several problems may occur: overall levels of anxiety may increase, anxiety reactions may generalize to other situations, and the overall symptoms become worse.

▶ Neurobiological theories

Extremely stressful events, or chronically high levels of stress, can also produce changes in the brain. According to neurobiological theories, *the system*—the brain and the body—react and change according to one's experiences. Some of the changes that veterans may be experiencing (e.g., increased irritability, sleep disturbances, hypervigilance) can be due to increased physiological reactivity. The associated neurobiological changes are covered more completely in Chapter 1. However, there are four important points to remember:

1. Among individuals who have survived extremely stressful events, parts of the brain (e.g., the amygdala) may begin to function differently—resulting in several physiological, emotional, cognitive, and behavioral changes for the individual, including their becoming more sensitive to cues that are interpreted as threatening.

2. Avoidance of cues that are not dangerous, but which cause anxiety, further trains the system to react to those cues as if they are dangerous, producing excessive anxiety and fear.

3. To help the person readapt to being back in a safer environment, it is important for them to resume more normal activities so that the system can re-tune itself to distinguish actual danger from other cues that may have become conditioned to produce a fear response.

4. Resuming normal activities also results in the person having more positive experiences overall, which can help to improve mood and overall level of functioning.

▶ Cognitive-behavioral theories

Cognitive and behavioral interventions can produce positive changes, both physiologically and psychologically. Cognitive and behavioral practice can help to create experiences that, over time, will result in the person being able to readapt following deployment—including helping their neurobiological system to reregulate—resulting in a reduction in stress reactions. Further, while the individual is working on reregulating the system, cognitive and behavioral skills can also help to manage and cope with aversive reactions. For example, relaxation skills and anger management skills can help a person negotiate difficult situations and reduce overall stress while working towards reducing their overall level of reactivity and anxiety.

The present intervention, which predominantly incorporates the use of cognitive-behavioral theories, trains the mind and body to better adapt to the level of anxiety or comfort appropriate to various situations. The next few sections address specific cognitive-behavioral techniques, which we adapt and utilize in our intervention.

■ Behavior modification techniques

Behavior modification theory purports that changing a client's behavior patterns—often with the use of reinforcement—will result in more adaptive functioning. Behavior modification techniques are used to directly alter a client's behavior patterns in order to minimize unhealthy coping behavior—such as habits that interfere with good sleep—and maximize healthy behavior—such as engaging in pleasant events. For example, sleep hygiene refers to a person's sleep-related habits. Numerous factors impact sleep quality, including use of caffeine, nicotine, alcohol and other drugs, anxiety, depression, stress, cognitive patterns, and exposure to light and darkness. Behavior modification techniques can be used to help clients make improvements in patterns of behaviors that impact sleep quality. In many cases, modification of behavioral patterns can strongly influence an individual's ability to develop and maintain adaptive functioning.

■ Cognitive modification techniques

It is important to recognize that typically our feelings and reactions (behaviors) are not direct responses to situations; rather, our reactions to situations are mediated by our *thoughts*. For example, Person A is at a social gathering and meets a coworker who is making little eye contact, frequently looks past him, looks around the room at other people, and glances at his or her watch several times. Person A might think, "wow, this person is really rude!" Alternately, Person B in the same situation might think to himself, "I must really be boring this person—they can't wait to go talk to someone else!" Person C might think, "I wonder if my coworker is waiting for someone—they must be preoccupied with finding a friend." Each of these thoughts likely results in feeling a different way about the situation.

The primary goal of many cognitive approaches can be viewed as assisting individuals to formulate thoughts and beliefs that are typically more realistic and adaptive, and by addressing a broad range of maladaptive thinking patterns. This includes training and practice focused on viewing stressors primarily as problems that can be analyzed and solved, rather than as potential dangers. With this model in mind, the therapist also takes on the role of a coach—assisting clients in a new type of training, with the end goal of helping the mind and body to readapt to the current environment (rather than it remaining adapted to the war environment).

Often our thinking, or cognitive process, occurs in a way that is unconscious and automatic. That is to say that our thoughts about situations arise very quickly and we may not be immediately aware that we are making numerous assumptions, appraisals, and attributions. The cognitive processes of individuals experiencing anxiety, depression, and traumatic reactions often include ruminations about potential loss, threat of danger, loss of control, self-blame, and cognitive attempts to undo decisions or events (Kubany, 1998; Resick & Schnicke, 1993).

Irrespective of the actual situation and the accuracy of the thoughts based on available evidence, these cognitive processes tend to be consistent with the person's mood (Bower, 1981) and tend to draw attention to things that support that thought. Another way of saying this is that these thoughts produce a confirmatory bias (Snyder, 1981) whereby they affect an individual's actual perceptions of events, making the beliefs stronger. Especially in people who have survived traumatic events, these maladaptive cognitive processes are often initiated quickly, frequently, and difficult to interrupt, and can become very resistant to information that challenges the thoughts (Meichenbaum & Deffenbacher, 1988).

■ Arousal reduction techniques

Returning veterans who have been in war may be experiencing problems such as insomnia, irritability, hypervigilance, or increased startle response symptoms of hyperarousal—a hallmark cluster of symptoms in Posttraumatic Stress Disorder. According to the respondent conditioning model, when an individual is exposed to an unconditioned stimulus, he or she can have a response that becomes conditioned and mediated by the autonomic nervous system (Follette, Ruzek, & Aubueg, 1998). Over time the individual will tend to experience generalized conditioned responses to other stimuli, which were previously perceived as being nonthreatening. Repeated, chronic over-reactivity of the autonomic nervous system can result in dangerous health consequences (Follette et al., 1998). Specifically, it can lead to headaches, back pain, chronic fatigue syndrome, hypertension, and other medical problems. Thus, it is imperative that veterans learn ways to undo the physical stress on their brain and their body vis-à-vis relaxation therapies and grounding techniques.

A very simple, yet effective skill for reducing arousal symptoms is *diaphragmatic breathing*—often called belly breathing. Veterans can learn how to breathe deeply and slowly from the diaphragm. When we breathe from our chests, we tend to take very shallow breaths. It is helpful to inform veterans that as they become more anxious or negatively aroused—as described previously—they tend to hyperventilate and feel more anxious. By appropriately using diaphragmatic breathing, veterans can slow their breaths down, which can create a sense of calm and well-being at the moment it is practiced. In addition, if veterans use this simple skill, they may feel less stressed and anxious with continued practice.

Other arousal reduction techniques may include progressive muscle relaxation, guided imagery and visualization, autogenic training, and self-hypnosis. To learn more about diaphragmatic breathing or other stress management and arousal reduction techniques, we recommend that you refer to books such as *The Relaxation and Stress Reduction Workbook* (Davis, Eshelman, & McKay, 2000).

■ Anxiety management techniques

Anxiety management can also utilize both cognitive and behavioral techniques. For example, Meichenbaum's (1985) stress inoculation training provides individuals with numerous tools for reducing anxiety, including:

1. Collecting information about specific anxiety-causing situations, and planning for appropriate resources and options;
2. Confronting and challenging maladaptive thoughts, such as all-or-nothing or catastrophic statements;
3. Using positive, accurate, adaptive self-statements;
4. Effective problem solving and assertiveness; and
5. Relaxation training.

These various skills are practiced prior to applying them in difficult situations, so as to gain proficiency and confidence that is then more easily translated into real-life contexts. To produce the best skill-acquisition in veterans, practice of new skills—where possible—is encouraged in three steps:

1. In session,
2. Out of session, in nonstress situations, and
3. Out of session, in stressful situations.

Rehearsal and practice of skills is critical, as each successful handling of a situation—each mastery experience—builds confidence for future situations. In addition to increasing mastery and confidence, successful application of skills can also boost motivation to continue using the same skill and learning and practicing new skills—as well as improving overall mood and helping to alleviate depressed mood.

■ Behavioral activation techniques

Behavioral activation is a structured way of helping a client to increase behaviors that are likely to be naturally reinforced, and that therefore will "produce corresponding improvements in thoughts, mood, and overall quality of life" (Hopko, Lejuez, Ruggiero, & Eifert, 2003). Basically, it is recognized that when individuals become depressed, they are less likely to engage in activities that are healthy, beneficial, effective, or rewarding. Essentially, when people do less, they end up having less energy overall, work and other tasks pile up causing more stress, they may feel increasingly guilty about their lack of activity and productivity, and they are doing fewer things that they enjoy. All of these things result in their feeling worse and the negative cycle continues.

The goal of behavioral activation is to break this cycle by encouraging individuals to do more activities that are likely to be rewarding because they produce success experiences, accomplish even small goals, are healthy and give the body more energy, involve positive social contacts with others, or simply because they are pleasurable. These activities—even if the person is having trouble enjoying them due to decreased mood—help to move the person towards being able to continue with more positive activities, creating a pattern of healthy improvement rather than continuing decline.

CHAPTER ONE

Understanding Transition Stress Reactions

The purpose of the first session is to help veterans understand typical responses to combat stress. Reactions to extreme stress—such as experiences associated with spending time in a combat zone—will be different for each individual. However, some elements of stress response are quite common and are likely to be experienced by most people at some point or another. Understanding typical responses often helps people to accept their own reactions without thinking that they are going crazy, or that no one else will understand what they are experiencing.

To fully appreciate that numerous combat stress reactions are typical responses to extraordinary stress (and *not* blameworthy, or indications of going crazy), it is important for veterans to understand that human bodies and brains are well designed to adapt to dangerous situations. Our bodies and brains will up-regulate at such times so as to become better able to detect danger and prepare us to deal with danger. Thus, we describe some of the basic neurobiological foundations of the stress reaction.

In this chapter, we also discuss how to recognize when transition stress reactions are beyond the expected responses and may need additional professional attention. In addition to helping veterans begin to understand some of the reactions they may be experiencing, this chapter includes some basic approaches to healthy coping and also provides background for learning the healthy coping behaviors that are discussed in the next chapter. We also provide a homework exercise to help veterans to begin reconnecting with others. This homework will also help veterans begin to monitor their own stress responses as they adapt to being back from war.

This book is designed to help promote the natural recovery of those who have returned from war. You know that coming home from the war zone *physically* may take a day or days, but coming home *mentally* is a process that can take weeks or months. Your retransition from the war zone is a period for the natural and gradual process of healing to take place.

Before battle, service members are provided with training and equipment to minimize or prevent physical injuries. When you were deployed to war, you used your military training to adapt to a dangerous, foreign environment. You used what

Col. Carl Castro calls your "Battlemind" to survive your hostile surroundings. Readapting to life outside of a combat takes a different type of training, and a different set of skills.

Resilient people have a set of tools that help them cope with and overcome the stressors in their lives. This program is designed to provide you with the training and tools you will need to retransition back from war. The transition home will be an ongoing, daily, and gradual process. Knowing what to expect puts you more in control of the recovery process.

▶ Understanding war-related stress

Post-deployment stress reactions are very common in those returning from prolonged combat deployments. The veteran may be coping with various acute stress responses—such as intrusive memories, nightmares, and strong feelings of agitation. It is helpful not to classify current stress at this stage as symptomatic, in the sense of being indicative of a mental disorder. Instead, it is important to recognize that these combat stress reactions are frequent, predictable, and typically transient reactions to extreme stress. In fact, about 60% of those who experience PTSD symptoms recover on their own, or with a little guidance (Resick & Schnicke, 1993).

Thus, rather than taking a pathogenic perspective, we begin the book by emphasizing a *resilience-wellness approach*. We help veterans understand that resilient individuals are able to withstand the negative impact of adversity and return to a healthy condition. Using this definition, the period of retransition is seen as a period for the natural healing process to take place. In this chapter, we help veterans to understand these reactions and begin to introduce healthy coping approaches. In Chapter Two, we teach specific tools for coping with combat stress reactions day-to-day.

Begin to normalize stress reactions for veterans. Also emphasize that over time the unpleasant reactions should decrease. Allowing veterans to see that such situations are typical of many veterans' reactions to the war zone helps them develop a stronger sense of control. Importantly, providing a plan of action for various reactions will increase their sense of self-efficacy, thus decreasing their levels of stress.

Our first course of action is to help you to understand some of the experiences you may be having following combat experiences. Each person's specific reactions to extreme stress will be different from other people's reactions. Some people may feel sad or numb, some may feel anxiety, and others may feel angry. Most people returning home will have a mix of many emotions, including gratitude and happiness. However, there are some types of reactions that are fairly common for people who have survived extreme situations such as a combat deployment.

■ Section A: Types of combat stress reactions

Take some time to address current combat stress reactions that veterans are experiencing. This is best done through a free-flowing conversation or discussion. This discussion is critical for veterans to begin developing an understanding of common responses to combat stress.

If a writing board is available, it may be useful to write down the symptoms described. It can be helpful to begin by writing the three symptom clusters—reexperiencing, hyperarousal, and avoidance/numbing—as headings so that specific symptoms or indicators can be grouped underneath the appropriate symptom categories. For example, when veterans suggest symptoms such as irritability, anger, and feeling jumpy or on guard, the symptoms can be written in the hyperarousal category. After the veteran has had an opportunity to describe some common symptoms that he or she may be experiencing, describe common reactions to combat stress.

There are several types of common reactions that the body and brain have following extreme stress (Resick & Schnicke, 1993). We are going to talk about four common reactions. One type of common reaction to extreme stress is called *reexperiencing*. Reexperiencing reactions include different ways that combat events may seem to repeat in our mind or body. Reexperiencing can include upsetting memories, thoughts, and images that come into your mind even when you are not trying to think about them, as well as dreams or nightmares about stressful events. Sometimes reexperiencing can occur when something reminds you of the stressful event. The reminders—sometimes called *triggers* or *cues*—can be many different things. Following war, a trigger may occur when veterans see people who remind them of the enemy, when they are in places that are similar to the war zone, or when they hear sounds or smell odors that remind them of their deployment. Reexperiencing often causes physical stress reactions in the body. For example, a person might experience a physical stress reaction (heart beating faster, sweating more, muscles tensing up, etc.) when something reminds them of a severly stressful event.

A second type of reaction includes the experience of being amped-up, also known as *hyperarousal*. Arousal is just energy or activation in the body. We all need some level of arousal or we could not get up and move around. Hyperarousal just means more arousal than we need, or more than is healthy or makes sense. Some veterans may feel like they have to be on guard all the time. They may startle following sudden noises and they may feel "jacked up" or "amped" a lot of the time. Some may feel very anxious or panicky. Some veterans find it hard to concentrate. They might be more irritable or angry than they used to. Also, veterans may have trouble falling asleep or staying asleep due to hyperarousal.

The third type of reaction following extreme stress is *avoidance*. Avoidance refers to going out of our way *not* to think about or to stay away from something. Because the other reactions—reexperiencing and hyperarousal—feel bad, some veterans try to avoid reminders of their deployment or anything that might trigger these other stress reactions. If a veteran feels uncomfortable in a shopping mall, he or she

CLINICIAN'S GUIDE TO TREATING STRESS AFTER WAR

might begin to avoid going to the mall. If a veteran is triggered by seeing people who remind him or her of the enemy, he or she may begin to avoid being around similar looking types of people. Veterans might try to avoid thinking about the war zone, or talking to people about it. Some people start to keep to themselves, or avoid watching TV or reading the news.

Related to avoidance, some people may experience *emotional numbing*, or may feel depressed. This can include having a hard time relating to other people or having a hard time trusting others. Veterans with emotional numbing may feel fewer positive feelings, like happiness. Often after stressful events people have a harder time enjoying things they used to, such as hobbies or going out with other people. Sometimes veterans lose their interest in food or sex, or may not be able to function sexually. Veterans may feel guilt related to things they did or did not do, such as making it back when others did not. After combat deployment, many people feel that they just don't have as much energy as they used to, or that their memory is not as good as it used to be.

After the veteran has identified reactions they—and others they know—are having, and these reactions have been discussed, it is useful to add a title to the list of reactions: common reactions to extreme stress.

So far we have been talking specifically about deployment-related stress. However, the reactions that we have discussed are not specific to veterans. These reactions are actually common reactions to extreme stress in general. Survivors of motor vehicle accidents, natural disasters, sexual assaults, and other crimes tend to have the same types of reactions. For example, two weeks after a sexual assault, 94% of rape survivors were found to have many of these reactions (Rothbaum et al., 1992).

Remember as we talk about these reactions to stress that we are talking about normal reactions that the body and brain have to very *extreme* events. Another way to say this is that they are normal reactions to an abnormal amount of stress.

■ Section B: Stress and the brain

This section on the neurobiology of traumatic stress response is critical for individuals to help them understand why they may be experiencing some of the reactions they are having. It also provides the background for the following section, regarding the role of avoidance in maintaining or decreasing adverse reactions.

Emphasize that the reactions that group members are experiencing are the result of body and brain reactions to extreme stress, and that these reactions are learned by the system (the body and brain). These changes are not innate—veterans were not born with them. Rather, they are the result of training and experience. As a result, they can also be changed through additional training and experiences.

To help understand why you may be experiencing some of the reactions that you have had, it is very important to understand how our system—meaning our brain and body—works to deal with danger. Our system is very efficient at helping us to detect possible threats and to prepare us to deal with those threats. When we have gone through extreme stress—such as almost being killed or seeing other people get seriously injured—our brain makes changes to become more attuned to danger. In the war zone, our system adapted to surviving in that environment. Parts of our brain actually adapt to be able to detect danger and keep you alive. Any time our brain detects possible danger it can fire the alarms and get us ready to act—to keep us safe.

The amygdala is a part of the brain's alarm system. The amygdala helps produce our emotions—including anxiety and fear (LeDoux, 2002). It is in charge of detecting danger, and then triggering the "freeze, flight, fight" system (Gray, 1988). Many of you may be familiar with the idea of fight or flight. But if we look at how our systems are really wired, the order is little different. First, when a serious threat is detected we are wired to freeze. Freezing protects us from predatory animals, which are very good at detecting movement. Second, the system is wired then to make us flee—to get away from the threat. Only when those options do not work or are impossible, are we wired to fight—as a last ditch effort to survive. Many veterans are embarrassed if they froze or ran when attacked or were in danger in the war zone. However, this is what we are wired for! Military training works to reverse this order, but it is hard to change biology.

It is important to strongly emphasize that the common understanding of the natural response to danger is incomplete. We often hear and think about it as fight or flight. However, more recent research outlines our actual natural wiring as "freeze, flight, fight, fright, faint"—recognizing that our complex system is truly designed to protect us and keep us alive. Training is sometimes effective in changing behavior, but under stress biology exerts a very strong influence. Also, many types of freezing and fleeing can occur—individuals may physically freeze, hide, or experience dissociation. As part of the central nervous system's sympathetic stress response, body functions change. Many changes occur as a part of this, including such things as tunnel vision, auditory exclusion, and bowel release. Although it is rarely talked about—and service members may be embarrassed if this happened to them in combat—bowel release is common and part of our natural physical reaction to danger (i.e., dysregulation of body functions that are not immediately essential to survival).

When we survive an extremely stressful situation, our alarm system (the amygdala) registers what is going on at the time—the temperature, the sounds we hear, the sights we can see, even the odors we smell. The amygdala registers all of these things as signs of danger. The problem is that once we are no longer in danger the amygdala interprets things we may have seen, smelled, heard, or felt as signs that danger is happening again.

When the brain detects something that it considers a sign of danger, the amygdala acts, and it acts fast. It's the amygdala's job to fire all of the alarms to the rest of the brain and body and prepare us to deal with danger. It throws adrenaline into the body, tenses the muscles, quickens the heart rate, stops digestion, and causes us to feel anxious, fearful, and on-guard. Basically, it prepares us for battle. When we have survived extremely stressful or dangerous situations, the amygdala can start to be overactive. That is why when veterans return from war, they often feel alarmed even when they are not in danger (LeDoux, 2002).

At this point it can be useful to give an example of the way that the amygdala associates cues with danger or conditions cues to indicate danger. For example, you can describe to the veteran a very detailed scene of walking down the street, including numerous details of the environment. If a traumatic event occurred—for example being hit by a car or attacked suddenly—then all of the environmental cues (including otherwise neutral or even pleasant cues) can be associated with danger, and can later cause the amygdala to fire the alarm, causing an anxiety or fear reaction. Some of the cues can be quite subtle—for example, innocuous sounds or smells, ambient temperature and humidity, even internal body sensations that occurred during the traumatic event (such as increased heart rate or respiration, tension in the muscles, feeling of dizziness, lightheadedness, or disorientation).

After returning from war, the amygdala often cannot tell the difference between what is really dangerous and what is not dangerous. It cannot tell Baghdad from the basketball court, Mosul from Mom's house, or Qandahar from a candy store. It seems to forget where we are, what year it is, sometimes even who is with us. So even though hot temperatures, or crowds, or enclosed places are not actually dangerous now, if you have been in dangerous situations like these in the past, the amygdala will assume you are in danger and will fire. And when it fires the "alarm," we do not just think, "maybe there's danger here." When our brain tells us something, we believe it. When the amygdala fires, we feel and believe that we are currently in danger.

After trauma, the amygdala changes our system so that the main goal is detecting danger and preparing to deal with danger. When the system has the main goal of detecting and dealing with danger, a lot of other things fall by the wayside. The amygdala tells us "you do not need to sleep—in fact sleeping will not keep you safe. I will keep you safe. Stay awake." It tells us "there is no need to enjoy your old activities—they will not keep you alive. No need to have a regular appetite, no need to feel close to other people, no need to feel sexual desire, no need to go out and enjoy life—those things will not keep you alive. I will keep you alive." As long as the amygdala is overactive, we can believe that we really are unsafe—no matter what is really going on.

Coming back from the combat theatre, you likely feel less safe than you did at home before you left. You may take more precautions now, and feel that the world has changed. However, believing we are unsafe does not actually make us safer—in fact, it can make us less safe. We will illustrate this with an example. If you are familiar with radar systems, you may know the idea of the "signal to noise ratio." The

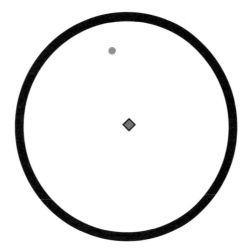

Figure 1.1   A radar system that is accurate or only slightly overactive.

signal to noise ratio is a measure of the amount of true information a radar detects (real threats) compared to false information or "noise." False information (or noise) is when the radar reports an object or threat when there is nothing dangerous there. Well-tuned radar will only register a threat when there is really something there— this is the optimal situation (see Figure 1.1). However, if the sensitivity of the radar is too high—maybe 1 or 2 percent—then you might get an occasional false blip. If the radar is too sensitive we might occasionally believe there is an incoming plane and scramble to intercept it—and find nothing is there. But, if the radar system is far too overactive you get constant blips on the radar (see Figure 1.2). Because every blip has to be investigated, we are constantly scrambling to check every signal. Of course this is very costly. It takes too many resources to check every possible threat. We become tired, overworked, and burned out. We do not know which blip is a real threat or if there is any real threat at all. Over time, the system gets overworked to the point that if a real threat does come, it is more likely to miss it.

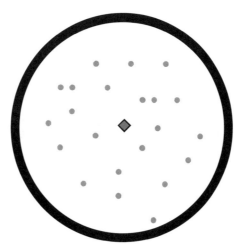

Figure 1.2   An oversensitive radar system.

■ Section C: The problem of avoidance

In this section, we discuss an extremely important and core component to our treatment model, and to the overall recovery process. Although it is certainly natural and understandable to avoid things that cause discomfort—or that trigger an anxiety or fear reaction—it is also critical to recovery not to avoid these things and to resume more normal activities. Indeed, it is critical to the system that the person does not avoid things that are safe, but that have become associated with fear or danger. This principle of nonavoidance—of resuming more normal activities so as to help the system readapt—will be a guiding principle throughout this program.

As mentioned previously, avoidance is when we go out of our way *not* to think about or to keep away from something. Trying to avoid reminders of highly stressful events is a natural reaction. For example, veterans who experience combat stress may try to avoid thinking about their war experiences. They may avoid talking about the war or not watch the news. However, there are a few problems with avoidance. First, there may be a lot of reminders around you, and it can be hard to avoid all the possible reminders.

There is another big problem with avoidance. Usually a lot of the things we are avoiding are things that were signs of danger in combat situations. For example, particular sounds or smells meant we needed to be ready to fight or get away quickly. The problem is that if we look at things here and now, we see that the same things we avoid are not signs of danger now. Our bodies and our brains are still avoiding cues for danger in the war zone—as if they still mean danger today.

If we avoid these reminders of the war zone, our bodies and brains do not get a chance to learn that the things that meant danger in the combat zone are not good predictors of danger here and now. When we avoid things that are not actually dangerous, we are taking away opportunities for the amygdala to learn. Even worse, the more we avoid, the more the amygdala becomes convinced that it really is dangerous.

To be able to get back to where you can go to places and enjoy doing activities you used to enjoy, you have to retrain the amygdala. There are two things that need to be done to overcome your stress reactions:

- For a while, you have to get used to the fact that even though the amygdala is firing the alarm there really is not any real danger there.
- For a while, you will have to allow yourself to feel *uncomfortable* when your amygdala is firing. To do this, you will have to allow yourself to tolerate reminders long enough and often enough—without avoiding them—so that your amygdala can learn that nothing bad is happening.

Accurate signs of danger *do* still exist. However, the cues from the war zone are not very good ones right here, right now. Right now the main thing old reminders do is to keep us really "amped" up and uncomfortable—rather than keeping us safe. Getting better means giving the amygdala enough new training so it relearns what the cues for real danger are, and stops triggering anxiety and fear when you do not need it. Now we will begin to teach you the tools you will need to manage your stress.

■ Section D: Monitoring stress

Everyone deals with stress in his or her own way. For this reason, it is important to know how *you* deal with stress. In this section, you will learn how to measure your stress levels and to use coping tools to manage your stress in different situations.

- Similar to checking the temperature in your home, we can measure stress level with a gauge. Instead of using a thermometer, the tool we use to monitor a person's stress level is the Subjective Units of Distress Scale (SUDS; Wolpe, 1973).

- The scale goes from 0 to 10, with higher numbers meaning more distress. A SUDS rating of 0 is the least stress you can feel—feeling no stress at all. On the other hand, if you are at a 10, you are so stressed that you can hardly stand it.

- Using the SUDS frequently is a very good way for you to know what is setting you off at a given moment in time.

- If your SUDS level goes above a 5, you should use a relaxation skill to calm yourself down.

On a scale of 0–10, with 0 being the lowest amount of distress you can feel and 10 being unbearable distress or anxiety, what is your SUDS level right now? Please circle the number that fits how you feel now.

Completely Calm

Nervous Wreck

0   1   2   3   4   5   6   7   8   9   10

■ Section E: Relaxation skills

Now that you have noted your SUDS level, you may be aware that you are feeling stressed. There are a number of skills you can use to calm your body and mind. One is called diaphragmatic or belly breathing. Try using belly breathing any time you feel upset, tense, or stressed out. With practice, it can help relax your body and distract you from what is bothering you.

Take some time now to try the relaxation skills below.

Diaphragmatic (belly) breathing

Something as simple as the way we breathe can help reduce stress. In general, we can say that most people do not breathe properly. We tend to rush our breathing, taking shallow breaths, from the chest. This is not an effective way of breathing. And when we get really stressed, we might even hyperventilate.

Have you ever noticed babies while they are sleeping? How do they breathe? When babies breathe in, their stomachs come out. When they exhale, their stomachs go flat. That is the proper way of breathing. As we get older and deal with life stress, we reverse the process. Adults usually breathe too shallow and too fast. What we want to do is to slow down our breathing to relax and to help our bodies be more efficient and not get overworked.

We are now going to teach a skill called diaphragmatic (belly) breathing. Belly breathing is a great tool to make us feel relaxed and calm. It helps our bodies to slow down and get more oxygen. This bodily change maximizes both our physical and mental abilities, so that we perform at our best. Best of all, belly breathing is very easy, quick, and useful in any situation. You don't need any equipment, and you can do it anywhere, practically anytime.

Before practicing belly breathing for a few minutes, please take a moment to write down your SUDS level before you start (see Figure 1.3):

SUDS: Before relaxation: _____ / 10

To practice belly breathing, sit comfortably in your chair with your hands resting on your stomach and your fingers laced together. Go ahead and take a nice deep breath in. As you do this, your stomach will come out and expand. Hold it for as long as it is comfortable. Then exhale very slowly—as you do, your belly will go back in and deflate. You can think of it as inhaling and filling your belly like a balloon gets filled with air—holding it for a few seconds, and then very slowly letting the air out of the balloon so that it deflates again. This may seem uncomfortable at first, but with a little practice it becomes a very useful relaxation skill.

If you want to, you can close your eyes and take a deep breath in, so your belly expands—hold for a few seconds—and then slowly exhale, so your belly goes in again. Then take another slow breath. Now, please practice belly breathing for at least three minutes. After three minutes, you should feel more relaxed. If you do not feel more relaxed, keep trying. Some people need a while to get the hang of it.

Now that you have practiced belly breathing, please take just a moment again to note your SUDS—estimating your level of distress on the scale from 0 to 10. Please write down your number here:

SUDS: After relaxation: _____ / 10

Hopefully you saw a decrease. If it's not that much of a decrease, do not be alarmed. It takes practice to get the numbers down. It is a skill that needs to be developed over time. Once you get it, you will know it—because you will feel much better.

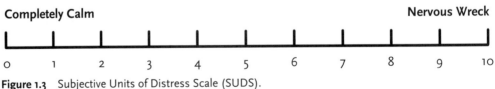

Figure 1.3 Subjective Units of Distress Scale (SUDS).

You will want to encourage veterans to try out different stress management and relaxation techniques. If you are not familiar with how to do the techniques, we have included resources for you at the end of this chapter. We recommend that you try these methods out yourself and become proficient with them. That way you will feel more comfortable and at ease as you teach them to your veterans.

■ Section F: Treatments for transition stress reactions

It is possible that you or someone you know are experiencing frequent nightmares, unwanted and distressing thoughts, images, or memories, hypervigilance, anxiety, depression, difficulty feeling positive emotions, or feeling very angry. If you are having any of these experiences, please know there is help available.

One of the most common treatments for these concerns is cognitive-behavioral treatment with a professional who is trained in dealing with stress reactions. A trained mental health professional helps to discover what might be setting off these reactions. He or she would then provide clear ways of dealing with these problems. It can also be very helpful to also work with a primary care physician or psychiatrist who can prescribe medication to help ease some of the symptoms.

▶ When to talk to your doctor

Have you or someone you know been:

- Avoiding people much of the time?
- Using drugs or alcohol more than normal or using them as an attempt to numb the pain inside or as the only way to relax or sleep?
- Feeling overwhelmed by your symptoms?
- Thinking of hurting yourself or someone else?

Did the veteran answer YES to ONE or more of these questions? If so, have them talk to their doctor right away.

▶ The heart of the matter

The transition from the war zone will be an ongoing, daily, gradual process. In this book, we provide you with the skills you will need to deal with reactions some people experience following war. We help you begin a plan of action so that you can be better prepared to cope with the transition back into civilian life. Use the SUDS to measure your stress level at least once per day. Then practice your new relaxation skills daily as well.

Brief quizzes are available at the end of each chapter (with answers in the Clinician's Guide *and at the back of the* Veteran's Workbook*). They can be used to evaluate the effectiveness of the material or simply to help veterans remember what they have learned.*

The veteran's copy of quizzes is provided at the end of the workbook as well as in Appendix D of this manual. Please remind veterans to review and complete the quiz.

- Please turn to the end of the chapter and take the quiz. The quizzes are a good way to review some of the important points in the chapter.

▶ Phone calling exercise

We include a Phone Calling Exercise as a useful way to help veterans to begin readapting and reconnecting with others. If treatment is in a group context, then this exercise can also help to begin building group cohesion (Ready et al., in press). There are several goals to the exercise, including helping veterans to connect as a group if in a group context, to begin reconnecting with others in general if in an individual context, and to begin reconnecting with others in a way that may be diminished following stressful military experiences. Further, this exercise provides an opportunity to discover that some experiences that are initially anxiety provoking (and may even cause a false alarm and fear response as discussed during this session) become much easier with practice, and may even become rewarding and enjoyable over time.

■ If treatment is in a group format

The exercise itself consists of each group member calling others in the group, asking each person a simple question, rating their own SUDS before and after making each phone call, and noting the duration of the call. Even though we ask veterans to write down the duration of the call, there is no required duration—we ask simply that they get an answer to their question from each member of the group.

Make a copy of the phone list at the end of this chapter, and prior to the end of the group session ask the veterans to write down their name, best telephone contact number, and the best times to reach them by phone. Compile this information, and give it to each veteran (e.g., by having each person write down the information on the same sheet and making copies for each veteran).

We provide Phone Calling Exercise Worksheets for veterans. Prior to the group, the clinician should prepare a question to assign to each veteran. Questions should be very easy at the beginning of the program, and may get a little more in-depth as time goes by and group members feel more comfortable with each other.

Questions may be as simple as:

- What was your first job?
- Do you have any pets?
- What is your favorite color?
- What is your favorite television show?
- What kind of music do you like?
- What is your favorite food?
- Who do you most admire?

- What was your favorite food when you were growing up?
- Who is your favorite actor/actress?
- What was the name of your best friend as a child?

By the fifth session, we recommend giving them blank forms and asking veterans either to make up their own questions to ask, or simply to make and write down the calls that they made. We typically want veterans to call about 6–8 people each week. If the group size is 10 or fewer, asking them to call each person in the group is beneficial. If the group size is larger, it is reasonable to ask the veterans to call 8 other members.

Veterans should be instructed that they should only ask their question if they initiated the phone call. When they receive a call, it is fine for them to immediately call the other person back afterwards, but part of the exercise is making the phone call itself.

■ If treatment is in an individual format

The same concept can be applied in terms of asking the veteran to call at least 5 individuals during the time between sessions. Of course, because the veteran will not be calling people who are also doing the exercise, they need not ask a specific question. In this case, the veteran should simply have to goal of calling 5 more people and speaking with them on the phone, noting their own SUDS before and after each call, as well as the duration of each call. The phone calls can be to people that they are in frequent contact with, or people with whom they have not spoken much recently. If it is more comfortable for the veteran, he or she can call for a specific reason—such as asking about details for an upcoming event. As with the exercise for the group format, as the treatment program progresses, the use of this exercise may also progress. For example, it may be useful later to ask the veteran to extend his or her phone calling to include individuals with whom he or she has been out of touch. In any case, the overall exercise involves the veteran reaching out by making phone calls to others.

▶ On your own

In the week ahead, try practicing belly breathing when you notice your stress level increasing. Take note of your SUDS level, then practice belly breathing for at least three minutes, then note your SUDS level. With practice, this relaxation tool will become more effective.

Additionally, isolating yourself from other people means losing support, friendship, and closeness with others, and more time to worry or feel hopeless and alone. Many veterans tend to isolate from other people to help avoid reminders and stress that goes along with talking to people. However, support from other people is one of the most important things to help you cope with combat stress. Therefore, one of the tools we will expect you to use is the telephone.

We would like for you make phone calls to others in the week ahead, to help you connect with other people. Complete the Phone Calling Exercise in which you call other people you know. Take the opportunity to talk to the other person for a few minutes.

Phone Calling Exercise

1. If you are part of a treatment group and were assigned a question, then follow the suggestions from your group leader. Ask your question when you call each group member and note each person's response. Remember that you should only ask your question if you initiated the phone call. When you receive a call, it is fine to call the other person right back after you have hung up.

2. If you are not part of a treatment group, set a goal for yourself to call five or more people in the next week. The phone calls can be to people that you frequently talk to, or to people that you have not talked to much recently. When you start practicing with this exercise, if it is more comfortable for you, you might call for a specific reason—such as asking about details for an upcoming event. As time goes by you may feel more comfortable making more calls. The important thing right now is to start reaching out by making phone calls to other people.

3. Using the Phone Calling Exercise Worksheet, write down your own SUDS before and after each call, as well as how long you are on the phone during each call.

4. Begin to practice using your belly breathing skills at least once a day during the coming week. Find a quiet place where you will not be disturbed. At first it is best to practice these skills when you are already feeling relatively calm. Like any other skill, it is hard to learn it under stress so practice when you do not need it at first. As you get better at using these skills, you will be able to use them more and more even under higher stress.

Remember that learning any new skill means taking the time and energy to practice and focus on learning. Also, as with trying anything new, it may feel a little weird at first. Keep practicing. Like many other skills you have practiced and gotten good at, with time you will get better and better. As you master each of the tools we provide in the workbook, they become easier to use, and more useful.

Phone List

Name	Best Phone Number	Best Times to Call

Phone Calling Exercise Worksheet

Name: _____

Session Number: _____

Question: _____

Person Called	Date	Your Own SUDS Before (0–10)	Answer/Topic	Call Length	Your Own SUDS After (0–10)

Cash, A. (2006). *Posttraumatic stress disorder: Wiley concise guides to mental health.* Hoboken, NJ: Wiley.

Davis, M., Eshelman, E. R., & McKay, M. (2000). *The relaxation and stress reduction workbook* (5th ed.). Oakland, CA: New Harbinger.

Foa, E. M., Keane, T. B., & Friedman, M. J. (2000). *Effective treatments for PTSD: Practice guidelines from the International Society for Traumatic Stress Studies.* New York: Guilford.

Friedman, M. J., Keane, T. B., & Resick, P. (2007). *Handbook of PTSD: Science and Practice.* New York: Guilford.

LeDoux, J. (2002). *Synaptic self. How our brains become who we are.* New York: Penguin.

Litz, B. T. (2004). *Early intervention for trauma and traumatic loss.* New York: Guilford.

Schnurr, P. P., & Green, B. L. (2004). Understanding relationships among trauma, posttraumatic stress disorder, and health outcomes. In P. P. Schnurr & B. L. Green (Eds.), *Trauma and health: Physical health consequences of exposure to extreme stress.* Washington, DC: American Psychological Association.

Name: _____

Date: _____ _____ / _____ _____ / _____ _____

1. What term refers to going out of our ways *not* to think about or to keep away from something.

    a. Hypervigilance

    b. Avoidance

    c. Reexperiencing

    d. Dropping out

2. It's very unusual to experience unwanted memories after returning from the war zone.

    True or False

3. Although reminders of stressful combat events can feel overwhelming, the reaction to reminders often lessens with time.

    True or False

4. Isolating from other people means loss of support, friendship, and closeness with others, and more time to worry or feel hopeless and alone.

    True or False

5. What does SUDS stand for?

    a. Strong Underpinnings of Denial and Suppression

    b. Subjective Units of Distress Scale

    c. The stuff you find floating at the top of beer

    d. Soap scum Under Da Sink

6. Working all the time to try to avoid distressing memories of the stressful event is a good way to deal with post-war stress.

    True or False

CHAPTER TWO

Managing Stress

When an individual undergoes stress over time, consistent, long-term changes occur in both the brain and the body. Long-term stress that is not managed can lead to changes in certain chemicals in the brain and interfere with optimal, healthy functioning. This means that a person under stress would have a more difficult time dealing with additional stress. Thus, managing stress is extremely important, particularly for veterans who are transitioning from the war zone.

In this chapter, we provide a review of common stress reactions, and describe positive and negative ways of coping with stress. We discuss the importance of monitoring one's level of stress, and teach positive ways of dealing with that stress.

In this chapter, we provide a review of common stress reactions, as well as positive and negative ways of coping with stress. We discuss the importance of monitoring one's level of stress, and we provide positive ways of dealing with that stress, including a description of what is called diaphragmatic (belly) breathing techniques. In this chapter you will learn a lot of ways to manage your stress.

Stress may either be acute or chronic. Acute stress can be a one-time incident that usually comes and goes quickly. Its effect on us can last from minutes or hours to days or weeks. Examples of acute stressors may include: narrowly avoiding an automobile crash, having a shouting match with someone, or taking incoming fire. Chronic or long-term stress tends to be the result of a continuing string of stressful incidences, or an ongoing situation. Examples of chronic stressors may include: caring for someone with a chronic disease, being in combat for months or years, dealing with chronic pain on a physical and emotional level, or trying to cope with ongoing emotional distress.

In Chapter 2, we focus on a thorough review and continuation of the two homework assignments: the telephone calling exercise and practice of belly breathing exercises. Strong emphasis on the review of the homework is critical. During this segment, through the review of the homework, we begin to emphasize several points:

■ Making positive changes requires changes in behavior and thoughts—to change, we have to think differently and do something different. The great philosopher and scientist Francis Bacon once said, "Things alter for the worst spontaneously, if they be not altered for the better designedly." William James said it this way, "To change one's life: 1. Start immediately, 2. Do it flamboyantly, 3. No exceptions." As veterans begin practicing the various homework exercises, they are more likely to see positive changes. Individuals who do not practice new behaviors and new habits are likely to experience no change (or, more specifically, no *improvement*).

■ Careful review of homework assignments, especially early in the program, sets the standard for completion of homework. By beginning each session with review of the homework, we help create a culture of full participation in the program. Ignoring the homework, or addressing it in a cursory way, conveys a false message that the homework is not important and that it is an optional part of the program.

■ Strong focus on the homework helps veterans to maximize the benefits that they can achieve during this program. Spending time examining individuals' experiences with the exercises, troubleshooting difficulties they encountered, and noticing successes they achieved, can help veterans to understand the critical role that they play in their own healing and growth. Conversely, failing to follow up on homework assignments sends the message that no effort is required for positive changes to occur. This is a recipe for treatment failure and poor outcomes.

■ Many of the strongest lessons occur as a result of veterans' practice of the homework. The actual amount of time that veterans will spend in the treatment itself is likely to be about 1–2 hours in a full week of 168 hours! While the core *information* is presented during the clinical session or group, the *practice* of the principles taught in this program are reinforced and learned in a powerful way by *putting them into practice*. Completing the homework exercises is critical to this process of incorporating therapeutic principles in a way that veterans can maintain, and from which they can continue to benefit, even after the completion of this program. For all of these reasons, it is essential during this session to carefully review each veteran's practice of homework exercises, and to encourage efforts made during the week.

HOMEWORK REVIEW: PHONE CALLING EXERCISE

■ Begin by reviewing the homework from the previous session.

■ Review the calls made as part of the Phone Calling Exercise:

—When calls were made

—If in a group context, the responses given by other veterans

—If in an individual therapy context, the types of topics discussed in the conversation (i.e., how the conversations went overall)

—The duration of the calls

—The caller's SUDS before and after the calls

—The caller's overall experience of the exercise

For group intervention format

■ If a person was not reached for a particular question, it can be useful to ask him what his answer to the question is—as well as asking people to answer their own. If this exercise is utilized in a group therapy setting, the group will hear a person's responses and veterans can begin to learn a little more about each other.

■ It can also be useful to discuss how they anticipated the exercise would go—and how it actually went. It is common for veterans to have numerous thoughts and expectations that engender anxiety about the exercise. Often they will think that it is silly or pointless, or that they simply do not want to do it. However, it is almost always the case that when individuals begin to reach out to others they open the door to more rewarding experiences, and they feel good about it. Especially when establishing contacts with others who may have shared similar experiences—or reestablishing connections with people with whom they have previously been close—the experience tends to be extremely positive. If appropriate, highlight differences between the anticipation of the Phone Calling Exercise and the actual outcome.

■ Thorough review of this exercise helps to reinforce the importance of the Phone Calling Exercise. Also, veterans may begin to notice that as they made more phone calls, the calls became easier. Some veterans may even report having begun to enjoy making phone calls.

Veterans' positive experiences with the Phone Calling Exercise serve as an excellent opportunity to discuss further changes that have occurred as a result of stressful events, especially reductions in social contacts, and at times strong isolation. It is common for many veterans to report enjoying the connection with other veterans during the phone calls. This will also later serve as an important example of the value of beginning to reengage in activities that veterans may have stopped doing, that they may want to avoid, or that they may feel are useless or pointless in comparison to their stressful service.

■ Provide ample encouragement and praise for efforts made in completing this exercise. It can be important to recognize that many veterans may have difficulty reaching out to others, and trusting others enough even to make phone calls to them. Beginning this homework exercise is an important step.

If some individuals did not complete portions of the homework exercises it is important to discuss and explore factors that interfered with their practice, as well as emphasizing the importance of daily effort in making positive changes. Remember that developing new habits takes effort, making changes takes time, and consistency is very important for retraining the system to adapt back to a more comfortable and efficient level.

HOMEWORK REVIEW: GROUNDING AND RELAXATION EXERCISES

■ Check in with each veteran regarding his or her practice of belly breathing techniques. Inquire as to whether they noticed any change in SUDS after their use of the techniques.

■ Explore what they noticed about their practice of various grounding techniques. Each veteran may prefer different techniques—it is important that veterans try a variety of approaches, and find specific grounding skills that are helpful for them.

It is often useful to teach veteran(s) one or more grounding exercises. Become comfortable with the practice of several skills, so that you can confidently lead the veteran(s) in the practice of these skills. When practicing grounding exercises in session, it can be helpful to demonstrate how individuals have the ability to lower their own SUDS using these exercises.

One way to do this is as follows:

- Ask the veteran(s) to think about a situation that is mildly upsetting. Ask them to focus on the details of such a situation—again, not something that is very upsetting, only annoying or irksome. Ask them to think about it for one minute.
- Poll each veteran for his or her SUDS after thinking about the mildly upsetting situation.
- Lead the veteran in the grounding exercise. Help the veteran to become engaged in the practice of the grounding exercise.
- Following the practice of the grounding exercise, again poll the veteran for his or her SUDS. Some individuals may notice a decrease in their SUDS even with this initial practice.
- Discuss with the veteran what happened as he or she practiced the grounding technique.

It is important to convey that as people get better at using the skill they can benefit from it much more and become able to use it in more stressful situations.

■ Section A: Unmanaged stress

When human beings endure too much stress and do not manage stress, the effects can be physical, emotional, and mental. For example, it is common for people returning from war to feel physically, mentally, and emotionally "on guard" and ready to take on anything dangerous.

Some common physical symptoms of stress include:

- Rapid heartbeat
- Headache
- Stiff neck and/or tight shoulders
- Backache
- Rapid breathing
- Sweating and sweaty palms
- Upset stomach, nausea, or diarrhea

Some common feelings and emotional symptoms of stress include:

- Feeling easily irritated or frustrated
- Losing your temper and yelling at others for no reason
- Feeling jumpy
- Being exhausted all the time
- Feeling ashamed or guilty
- Feeling anxious or worried

Some common symptoms of stress include:

- Finding it hard to concentrate or focus on tasks
- Thinking too much about insignificant things
- Doubting your ability to do things
- Having problems remembering things
- Believing you are missing opportunities because you cannot act quickly

Below, you will find the Identifying Stress Cues Worksheet. Please take a moment and fill it out. This will help you understand how you respond to stress.

Identifying Stress Cues Worksheet

A very important part of monitoring our stress is to identify how we react to things that happen in our lives. These are cues because, if we pay attention to them, we will be able to know that we are in a high-stress situation. Please fill out each section below so that you can become more aware of what your own particular stress cues are, and what sets you off and stresses you out.

1. Physical cues (how your body responds to stress, i.e., increased heart rate, tightness in chest, upset stomach, feeling hot):

_____

_____

2. Feeling and emotional cues (feelings that come up, i.e., fear, anger, sadness, guilt):

_____

_____

3. Thinking and mental cues (what we think about in response to the event, i.e., negative self-talk such as "I'm going to lose control," "I've got to get out of here," "I can't handle this"):

_____

_____

It is not unusual for returning warriors to maintain beliefs that support keeping extremely high levels of stress and hypervigilance. If discussion in session has revealed these beliefs, it may also be useful to confront the idea that high levels of stress are completely adaptive.

It is important to validate veterans by recognizing that their bodies adapted well to combat by learning how to maintain high levels of arousal over extended periods, that it is very difficult and uncomfortable to feel constant anxiety, and that they may still often feel unsafe even in their current environment. It is important for the clinician to accept that a change in perceived level of safety is part of the expected reaction to combat stress and that it may take much more time before veterans begin to feel safer. One goal of this section is for the veteran to begin to develop the skills to better control their level of stress and distress in situations that they feel may be safer—and hopefully these sessions are one of those places.

It is common for veterans to return from their service in-country feeling amped or on-guard most of the time. And of course it is important to be able to develop this kind of mode—while you were in-country, you absolutely needed to stay "on" most, if not all, of the time. Your safety, your life, and the lives of others around you relied on your being ready for anything to happen. We often believe that being hypervigilant—that is, keeping a high level of alertness—is essential to keep us safe. We tell ourselves that staying all the way keyed-up makes it more likely that we will be able to respond to whatever situation comes up.

In the last section, we discussed the reality that a moderate level of arousal is more efficient and safer than hyper-arousal. The same is true for stress (see Figure 2.1). Although a moderate level of stress helps us to handle situations, once our stress level gets too high, we are actually *less* ready to handle difficult situations. As you can see in Figure 2.1, when we have a moderate level of stress, we are at our peak physically, emotionally, and mentally.

When our body is too amped-up, we miss important details, misinterpret situations, make poor judgments, and perform less well. Also, over time stress wears us out and makes it less likely that we will be able to respond to situations accurately and quickly. Over a long period of time, stress wears down our body and weakens our immune systems—making us more likely to get a number of diseases. Once the initial threat is over (i.e., after a deployment), we have a choice. It is much healthier and safer for us to bring our overall stress level down.

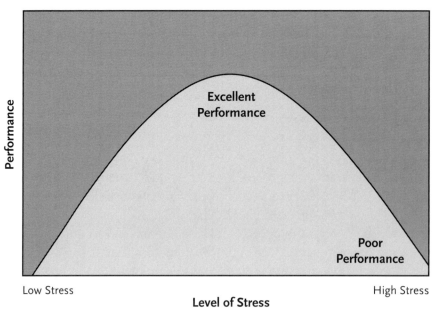

Figure 2.1 We perform best at a medium level of stress. With too little stress, we may not be motivated, but too much stress interferes with our functioning.

■ Section B: Coping with and managing stress

In addition to feeling stress associated with deployment to a combat zone, veterans often also feel stressed about their reactions to how they are handling everything.

Check in with the veteran and ask him or her what kinds of things they do to calm down and manage stress. For example:

■ What kinds of things do you do to calm down and decrease your stress level?

There are a number of ways to manage your stress. You already learned how to identify how stressed you feel (i.e., with SUDS described in Chapter 1 and the Identifying Stress Cues Worksheet in this chapter). Now we are going to discuss some of the most important tools that you can use to de-stress. These are mind-centered and body-centered exercises. *Mind-centered exercises* are stress management skills that focus on calming your mind. Some mind-centered exercises include:

■ Meditation (including mindfulness meditation)
■ Prayer
■ Visualization
■ Self-hypnosis
■ Autogenic training
■ Music therapy

Each of these skills can be used to help calm your mind, which can also relax your body and decrease your stress. There are a number of *body-centered exercises,* which are stress management skills focused on your body. These include:

■ Diaphragmatic (belly) breathing
■ Progressive muscle relaxation
■ Massage
■ Aromatherapy
■ Yoga, Tai Chi, or Qi Gong

These exercises calm your body and your emotions. They are very useful skills to help you to feel more relaxed and less stressed.

Now let's try another body-centered exercise. First, on a scale of 0–10, with 0 being the lowest amount of distress you can feel and 10 being unbearable distress or anxiety, what is your SUDS level right now? Please circle the number that fits how you feel now (see Figure 2.2).

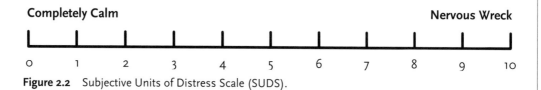

Figure 2.2 Subjective Units of Distress Scale (SUDS).

It is very important that you normalize their combat stress reactions. Let them know that what they are experiencing is expected, considering what they have been through. There is nothing wrong with them. It is very common for returnees to have a lot of different emotions. You might say, for example: "What you are feeling right now is expected, especially given what you have been through."

Here is another example of a relaxation tool called Progressive Muscle Relaxation (or PMR). Try using PMR breathing at least once a day to help keep your stress level down. With practice, it can help relax your body and promote better functioning. Begin by lying on your back or sitting in your chair in a comfortable position.

- If you are lying down, allow your arms to rest at your sides, palms down, on the surface next to you. If you are sitting, rest your hands on your lap.
- Inhale and exhale slowly and deeply.
- Clench your hands into fists and hold them tightly for 15 seconds. As you do this, relax the rest of your body. Visualize your fists contracting, becoming tighter and tighter.
- Then let your hands relax. On relaxing, see a golden light (like the sun) flowing into the entire body, making all your muscles soft and pliable.
- Now, tense and relax the following parts of your body in this order: face, shoulders, back, stomach, pelvis, legs, feet, and toes. Hold each part tensed for 15 seconds and then relax your body for 30 seconds before going on to the next part.
- Finish the exercise by shaking your hands and imagining the remaining tension flowing out of your fingertips.

MIND-CENTERED ACTIVITIES

Mind-centered activities help relax the mind and are often combined with body-centered relaxation exercises. They include:

- Autogenic training, Self-hypnosis, and Meditation (including mindfulness meditation) focus your attention on feeling calm and having a clear awareness about your life.
- Guided imagery (visualization) is a method of using your imagination to help you relax and release tension caused by stress.
- Music therapy can relax your body, improve your mood, and change the pace of your day through listening to different types of music.

BODY-CENTERED EXERCISES

Body-centered relaxation skills that help the body relax are useful for those who experience mainly physical symptoms of stress. These are especially good techniques for individuals that hold their stress or tension in their bodies. These skills include:

- Breathing exercises, such as belly breathing.
- Progressive muscle relaxation, which reduces muscle tension by relaxing individual muscle groups.
- Massage, such as a shoulder and neck massage.
- Aromatherapy, which uses the aroma-producing oils (essential oils) from plants to promote relaxation.
- Yoga, Tai Chi, and Qi Gong, which are forms of exercise and meditation. They generally require initial instruction to learn how to practice safely and effectively.

Now take another moment to note your SUDS level after having practiced this skill. Does your body feel more relaxed? How much more relaxed? How much calmer do you feel afterward?

Skills improve with practice. Relaxation is no different. We must practice the skills to perfect them—to be able to automatically recall them when we need them most—such as when we are really stressed out. A perfect example is when we learn self-defense or combat tactics. The more you practice them, the more they become ingrained so that you can recall them instantly in a time of need. The same holds true for relaxation therapies. They should be practiced often for their usefulness in producing helpful and lasting results. Remember that like any new skill or way of doing things, it may feel funny or strange at first when you practice these relaxation skills. Remind yourself that the feeling of strangeness will decrease as you practice it, and your ability will increase. Stick with it long enough so that you become skilled, so that you will feel more relaxed and in control of your body's reactions.

■ Section C: Treatments for stress and anxiety

Treatments for anxiety and stress generally start with examining what causes a person to feel stressed or anxious. Once the cause(s) of stress are identified, the person can then work with their mental health professional and doctor to identify the best way(s) to manage that stress. Common treatments for managing stress include: biofeedback, body awareness training, and the other coping skills we talked about in this chapter. If you are unable to reduce your stress using the skills in the chapter, consider seeing your doctor. Some medications may also be helpful to help calm that anxiety in the short-run.

▶ When to talk to your doctor

Have you or someone you know been:

- Experiencing your heart racing, headaches, backaches, or having an upset stomach pretty frequently?
- Feeling exhausted or overwhelmed?
- Feeling like you might hurt yourself or someone else?

Did the veteran answer YES to ONE or more of these questions? If so, have him or her talk to their doctor right away.

▶ The heart of the matter

In this chapter, we spoke about common stress reactions that you may be experiencing now—since returning from war. There are both positive and negative coping reactions to stress. It is important that we check ourselves and monitor our stress levels. One way of doing this is by using the SUDS level to measure distress at least one time per day. By monitoring our stress and knowing what triggers us, we are more apt to use positive coping to deal with that stress. There are numerous body-centered and mind-centered ways of improving the ways that we manage stress. As with any new skill, relaxation skills need to be practiced again and again, so that we can remember how to use them when we need to.

Remember to ask veterans to complete the quiz at the end of the chapter. The quizzes are a useful way to review content from each section and help veterans focus on new skills and ideas they learned during the session.

- Please turn to the end of the chapter and take the quiz. Remember that the quizzes are a good way to review some of the important points in the chapter.

▶ Phone calling exercise

As with the previous chapter, assign the Phone Calling Exercise. If treatment is in a group context, it is useful to provide a question to each veteran to help facilitate the calling and give a starting point for the call.

▶ On your own

1. Complete the Phone Calling Exercise Worksheet in the same way that you did for the last session. Remember to note your SUDS before and after each call. Complete details about this exercise are included in the On Your Own section at the end of Chapter 1.

2. Use the Weekly Stress Monitoring Worksheet so you can know what sets you off and increases your stress. Awareness is key to producing changes.

3. Practice PMR and belly breathing at least one time per day in the next week. Write down what days and times you are able to practice that skill on the Weekly Stress Management Schedule at the end of this chapter.

You are on your way to managing your stress level! Remember you must practice these skills every day to keep your stress level down. Any time you feel guilty about taking the time to do this, remember that *your effort will be worth it.*

Phone Calling Exercise Worksheet

Name: _____

Session Number: _____

Question: _____

Person Called	Date	Your Own SUDS Before (0–10)	Answer/Topic	Call Length	Your Own SUDS After (0–10)

Weekly Stress Monitoring Worksheet

Use this sheet to record your stress during the week. You can still use this worksheet in session to discuss what occurred that caused your stress to rise, and what you did to manage the stress reaction. This can also be used to help you develop additional strategies to deal with similar situations in the future.

1. For each day this week, monitor and record the highest number you reach on the Stress Meter.

   _____ Monday

   _____ Tuesday

   _____ Wednesday

   _____ Thursday

   _____ Friday

   _____ Saturday

   _____ Sunday

2. What was the highest number you reached on the Stress Meter during the week?

   _____ / 10

3. What type of events triggered your stress?

   _____

   _____

   _____

4. What cues were associated with the stress-inducing event?

   Physical Cues _____

   _____

   Feeling Cues _____

   _____

   Thinking Cues _____

   _____

5. What strategies did you use to prevent hitting a 10 on the Stress Meter (assuming you did not hit a 10)? _____

   _____

Stress Management Schedule

Write down what times you will practice at least one stress management skill in the week ahead. Try to practice at least one technique per day. Put this schedule some place in your home where you will see it often—such as your refrigerator door, bathroom mirror, or nightstand.

	Monday	Tuesday	Wednesday	Thursday	Friday	Saturday	Sunday
0600 hrs.							
0700 hrs.							
0800 hrs.							
0900 hrs.							
1000 hrs.							
1100 hrs.							
1200 hrs.							
1300 hrs.							
1400 hrs.							
1500 hrs.							
1600 hrs.							
1700 hrs.							
1800 hrs.							
1900 hrs.							
2000 hrs.							
2100 hrs.							
2200 hrs.							
Night ↓							

▶ Further readings for the clinician

LeDoux, J. (2002). *Synaptic self: How our brains become who we are.* New York: Penguin.

Meichenbaum, D. H. (1985). *Stress inoculation training.* New York: Pergamon.

Name: _____

Date: _____ _____ / _____ _____ / _____ _____

1. What are some common symptoms of long-term stress?
   a. Irritability
   b. Upset stomach, nausea, diarrhea
   c. Stiff neck or headaches
   d. All of these are common

2. Which of these are **positive ways** to cope with stress?
   a. Exercise
   b. Driving fast in your car
   c. Drinking a case of beer
   d. All of these are a positive way to cope with stress

3. Which of these are **negative ways** to cope with stress?
   a. Obsessing or worrying about things
   b. Smoking weed
   c. Road raging
   d. All of these are not good

4. What would be an example of a **mind-centered** stress management skill?
   a. Guided imagery
   b. Self-hypnosis
   c. Autogenics
   d. All of these are mind-centered skills

5. This is a relaxation skill where you breathe in with your belly coming out, and exhaling and your belly coming back in. It is very easy and helps people to relax. What is it called?
   a. Autoreflex breathing
   b. Deep muscle breathing
   c. Diaphragmatic breathing
   d. Exhalation Therapy

CHAPTER THREE

Tools for Healthy Coping

The purpose of this session is to encourage healthy coping behaviors aimed to increase resilience in veterans. Individuals who are depressed or suffering from combat stress are less likely to engage in activities that are rewarding. In this chapter, we incorporate Lewinsohn, Hoberman, and Hautziner's (1985) work with depressed clients to help veterans understand the connection between healthy coping activities and positive mood. We introduce behavioral activation techniques as a way of helping veterans break the downward spiral of depression (Beck, Rush, Shaw, & Emery, 1979). Behavioral activation is an effective treatment for depression (Hopko, Lejuez, Ruggiero, & Eifert, 2003) and has been found to outperform cognitive therapy in the treatment of severe depression (Dimidjian, 2006). Such methods enable veterans to engage in behaviors that will make them feel useful and capable, and that are otherwise naturally rewarding. When individuals take direct action to cope with their problems, they put themselves in a position of power and start to feel less helpless.

In this session, we will talk about and develop a plan to start using healthy coping activities that help people build their own resilience. These coping tools will help us become better able to deal with the effects of stressful events and continue a healthy recovery. Healthy coping activities are different for different individuals, but all of them help people to tolerate stress reactions and decrease the risk for depression. It is important to stay active in addressing problems as they come up—when we take direct action to cope with our problems, we keep ourselves in a position of power so that we feel stronger and less helpless.

▶ Review of homework

Review the Phone Calling Exercise in a similar fashion to the previous session. Often it makes sense to be somewhat briefer with the phone calling review during this session, especially if the veteran has connected well with this particular homework, and is having an easier time with it.

Review

- When calls were made
- Responses to questions (for group therapy assignment), or topics discussed (individual therapy context)

- The duration of the calls
- The caller's SUDS before and after the calls
- The caller's overall experience of the exercise

Review the veteran's the Weekly Stress Monitoring Schedule. Discuss stress management approaches that they opted to utilize, and what they noticed about this practice. Help to problem-solve difficulties in implementing stress management techniques and provide ample encouragement for efforts made in this area.

If some individuals did not begin practicing new coping strategies since the last session, you may choose to focus on factors that interfered with practice—as well as emphasizing the importance of daily practice.

■ Section A: Reactive and proactive coping tools

First of all, let's talk about coping strategies. There are two types of tools that are important in an overall plan for effective coping:

- *Reactive coping tools* are skills and behaviors that we do in response to a problem. Like firefighters responding to a fire in progress, reactive strategies are focused on reducing or removing a problem that is already there. If you are stressed and use belly breathing to help calm yourself down, you are using a reactive coping tool.

- *Proactive coping tools* are behaviors that we do to prevent problems from taking place or to prepare ourselves to better handle possible problems that might occur in the future. These include skills and habits that improve our overall health, making us more capable of handling stresses in general. This also includes practicing and mastering skills when we do not immediately need them (for example, practicing relaxation skills when you're already feeling pretty relaxed) so that we get better and can use the skill when we most need them (and when they are hardest to use). Many of the skills and activities that we will discuss in this chapter are proactive coping skills.

After describing the two types of coping strategies, discuss examples of each type. Proactive coping strategies include both practicing coping tools during calm times (preparing for when they are truly needed), as well as promoting overall healthy habits.

- So the ideas we focused on last week—and the coping skills you practiced as your assignment—are ways of practicing reactive coping tools. It is very important to practice some of these even when things are going well, so that you develop your skill for when you most need them. Of course you are already familiar with this type of learning from your military training—where you learn a skill first at a basic level and practice it over and over—so that you are able to do it almost automatically.

- We can use the same principle to help with healing now. For example, to learn relaxation training, the best way to improve is to practice every day—even if it seems like you do not really need it. That way you are better able to use it when you are really stressed—even when you get really amped—because you have practiced the skill so well.

The skills that we will be focusing on during this session are more proactive skills, which include overall health coping behaviors.

People vary in the ways they deal with stress. This is called one's *coping style*. Some people can be more prone to take action in times of stress; others tend to be very reflective and study the situation. And others tend to become reserved, not doing much in times of stress.

Similarly, different people enjoy different kinds of activities. Some people like walking in the woods, others like wild parties with lots of people. Some people like building models or working on engines, while others like taking pictures or painting landscapes. Others like running, or working out. When it comes to healing and readapting to being back home, the best healthy coping behavior is the one that you will make a commitment to doing on a regular basis.

In the following section, we explore the importance of healthy coping activities. We also look at types of activities that are especially likely to make people feel good. We start by describing how *not* engaging in coping activities can lead to negative outcomes, such as depression.

■ Section B: Depression and the danger of doing nothing

Over the years, researchers have studied why people feel depressed and what drives depression for various individuals. For example, some studies have shown that when someone has negative thoughts, they are more likely to become depressed (Seligman, 1991). Studies also conclude that when people focus too much on themselves and blame themselves for their problems, they have more depression.

When we have negative thoughts that automatically pop up in our minds, this can lead to negative feelings such as sadness or anger. And these thoughts and feelings can lead to negative beliefs about other people, our futures, and ourselves. Negative thoughts, feelings, and beliefs also all lead to depression (Beck, 1995). We know—based on research—that negativity can breed more negativity, and this can be a vicious cycle for a person. In fact, it can lead to a "downward spiral of depression," (Lewinsohn et al., 1985) which means that someone who thinks, feels, and believes in a very negative way will feed negativity, and they will become more and more depressed over time (see Figure 3.1). Basically, this is what can happen:

■ When people have depressed *feelings,* they may have discouraging *thoughts,* and are less likely to do the things (engage in *behavior*) that might make them feel better. This leads to even greater depression, which in turn leads to more discouraging thoughts that then lead to more inactivity.

■ Additionally, war injuries and/or chronic pain may be keeping us from doing the kinds of activities we used to do to have fun or to feel better.

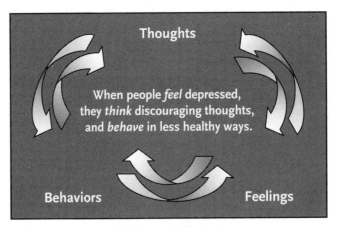

Figure 3.1 Interactions among thoughts, feelings, and behavior.

- When we are doing very few activities, we are more likely to feel depressed. Also, when we feel depressed, we do not feel like doing the kinds of activities that are likely to help us out of depression.

- When we are depressed or feeling out of sorts, we are least likely to do the things that we need the most—the things that are most likely to help us feel better. This is known as the *downward spiral of depression* (see Figure 3.2). It becomes a dangerous, vicious, negative spiral.

Depression keeps us from doing activities that once were fun and healthy for us. Physical injuries may make it even harder for us to do things we used to enjoy. However, the less we do, the more depressed we feel. The more depressed we feel, the less we feel like doing anything.

■ Section C: Negative coping, negative mood

Some things that people do to try to cope can actually make their mood worse. These *negative coping responses* can be anything that does not bring us what is really good for us in the long run. Even though we might be doing these coping activities to try to feel better, the reality is that people who use negative ways of coping usually feel worse. They usually feel angrier, more upset, and more depressed. Here are examples of negative coping responses:

- Criticizing yourself (negative self-talk)
- Driving too fast in your car
- Becoming aggressive or violent (hitting someone, throwing, or kicking something)
- Eating too much or too little, or drinking a lot of caffeinated beverages
- Smoking or chewing tobacco
- Drinking alcohol or taking recreational drugs
- Yelling at your spouse or partner, children, coworkers, or friends

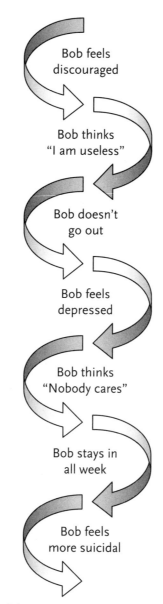

Bob feels
discouraged

Bob thinks
"I am useless"

Bob doesn't
go out

Bob feels
depressed

Bob thinks
"Nobody cares"

Bob stays in
all week

Bob feels
more suicidal

Figure 3.2   The downward spiral of depression.

■ Avoiding social contact

■ Dropping out of recreational activities

■ Working long hours to avoid thoughts or people

Because each of these negative coping strategies has some allure—meaning that it is rewarding in some way—it can be important to address some of these and highlight the obvious, as well as the more subtle problems that each can cause. Specifically, most of them actually prevent healing in some way. For example, some veterans may say that driving recklessly—as well as other reckless, thrill-seeking, or adrenaline-seeking behaviors—are the only ways that they "feel alive."

Indeed, if they have adjusted to an environment of constant stress, returning to the normal world may be boring in many ways. However, continuing to seek the adrenaline rush in destructive ways—in addition to the obvious dangers—can also prevent the amygdala, as well as other parts of the system, from readapting to normal circumstances. Similarly, many veterans may avoid social contacts or other recreational activities because they do not feel safe or comfortable in many contexts. However, avoiding these situations also slows down or prevents their healing by depriving the system of opportunities to learn that these situations are safe.

Negative coping behaviors can lead to a downward spiral. Fortunately the opposite is also true—there is also a *positive spiral*. The more positive coping we do, the less depressed we feel, and the less depressed we feel, the more we will feel able to do things. Getting your post-deployment lives back on track will involve making the effort to start doing the things that will break the downward spiral.

■ Section D: Positive action, positive mood

Positive coping behaviors break the downward spiral by helping individuals to do more activities that are going to improve their mood. And as people begin to incorporate more of these positive behaviors into their life, the positive coping begins to make them feel better and to give them more energy. So in addition to beginning to feel better, it also becomes easier to do more positive behaviors, and the benefits begin to multiply.

Again, our goal is to begin practicing more activities that result in decreased stress and anxiety—as well as better overall mood and better overall health. Even if you are having trouble enjoying the activities at first, these activities help to move you towards a better mood and better energy—and being able to continue with more positive coping habits. This can help to create a pattern of healthy improvement, rather than continuing decline. Here are some positive ways of dealing with stress, and promoting better health and coping:

Positive Coping Responses

- Playing with children, your spouse or partner, or a pet
- Writing, painting, or other creative activity
- Praying or going to church
- Exercising or getting outdoors to enjoy nature
- Listening to positive music
- Laughing or crying
- Going out with a friend (playing golf, going to a movie, going bowling, going out to dinner)
- Taking a relaxing bath or shower
- Discussing situations with a spouse or partner, or close friend
- Gardening or making home repairs

- Singing or dancing
- Practicing deep breathing, meditation, or progressive muscle relaxation

Describe the impact of positive (adaptive) and negative (maladaptive) coping responses. Using an interactive style, discuss examples of each style of coping. Remind the veteran that consistent use of positive coping strategies is a critical part of an overall proactive coping system.

We all find ways of coping with stress. Some coping methods are helpful, while others are harmful and can make the problems much worse. For example, an individual who chooses to do some deep breathing and meditation will gain a sense of calmness, peace, and decreased anxiety. Positive or healthy coping tools result in decreased stress and depression, and help promote better health over time. On the other hand, someone who chooses to keep going over their worries will become more anxious, uptight, and helpless.

Evaluate whether the veteran is using mainly positive or negative coping strategies. If they are utilizing negative coping, do not reinforce this. Instead, point out that they have done the best they have been able to do up to this point, and that now they may be able to develop better ways to deal with stress in the future, for example:

- Okay, I want to emphasize that you have done the best you could have up until now. When you know more, you can do better. So, now we can come up with improved ways of coping with stress. Let's try to figure out what those ways might be for you.

Types of positive coping activities

Now we are going to get more specific. In this section, we provide you with a summary of three categories of things you can do to help you feel better—things that will help prevent stress and depression.

Category one: Body-focused activities

Body-focused activities can be a great way to decrease levels of stress and depression, and increase energy. Many of these exercises reduce chemicals in the body associated with stress and increase chemicals that produce good feelings, helping to promote overall good health and mood.

Mind/Body exercises focus on helping the body to better handle stress. They are all focused on relaxing or focusing our energy in a more positive and healthy way, or both.

Physical Exercise

- Going for a walk
- Bicycle riding

- Swimming
- Lifting weights
- Hiking
- Playing a sport with someone
- Kayaking
- Surfing
- Jogging or running
- Doing yard work
- Cleaning house

Mind/Body Exercises
- Diaphragmatic (belly) breathing
- Progressive muscle relaxation
- Massage
- Aromatherapy
- Yoga
- Tai chi
- Qi Gong
- Meditation
- Pilates
- Autogenics
- Hypnosis

Category two: Goal-focused activities

We all need to feel useful and productive. Setting positive goals and achieving them is an excellent way to improve mood and decrease depression. Achieving something can include:

- Learning a new skill
- Starting on a new project
- Cleaning out the closet
- Organizing your bills
- Planning an event
- Solving a problem at-hand
- Fixing something that is broken
- Taking a class
- Learning a new language
- Learning to play an instrument

Category three: Social activities

As we have discussed, often following highly stressful events, such as military deployments, people are inclined to isolate themselves from others. However, resisting this urge to isolate and instead increasing social activities provides us with support. Being with others also helps our brain and body begin to re-regulate and re-adapt to being back home—social activity is good for the brain. Also, social activities create more opportunities for us to experience positive interactions with others.

- *Talking with others:* Call family members or talk to a close friend who you trust. Talking with a person with whom you feel safe (a family member, friend, spouse or partner, clergy, therapist, etc.) helps us feel understood, and it helps us see things a little differently sometimes.

- *Spending time with others:* Join a social club, invite someone over, have coffee or play cards with your friends, play a team sport, go to a party, make new friends, take someone on a date, play with a pet, or just sit and watch other people.

- *Helping others:* Volunteer to help others, such as at a hospital, nursing home, soup kitchen, or homeless shelter. Help friends or family members, visit someone who is lonely, spend time with children or the elderly, or help organize or coach a team. When we provide service to others, it can help us to focus our mind on positive action and can help others accomplish things they could not have done otherwise.

Category four: Other positive activities

There are numerous other activities that have been shown to help reduce stress and promote better health and better mood. Some other examples include:

- *Writing or journaling:* Writing letters, stories, poetry, or writing in a journal can help improve well-being and lower people's risk for disease. Writing 10–15 minutes a day about stress in your life especially can lower your stress level quite a bit.

- *Going out:* Plan a trip, take a drive, go fishing, go to a concert, a fair, the zoo, a restaurant, a park, a museum, or to the beach.

- *Laughing and crying:* Laughing and crying are natural ways to relieve stress and release tension. They are both part of the emotional healing process. Tell a joke, laugh at a comedy, or cry during sad movies. All of these can be excellent ways to help release stress. Even though we often think that we should not cry, or that it is a sign of weakness, the reality is that crying is an important and natural part of the overall grieving process, and can be part of getting better.

- *Create something:* Draw a picture, paint a painting, write or play music, make crafts, do yard work or decorate your house.

- *Try a hobby:* Build a model, take up photography, learn to cook, read a book, collect baseball cards, or something that is meaningful to you.

- *Be spiritual:* Pray, join a house of worship, talk with others about ethics or religion, go to a religious service, read sacred works, listen to a sermon, or participate in church groups.
- *Do something fun:* Go boating, hiking, camping, swimming, or diving, toss a ball or Frisbee, play chess, checkers, dominoes, or another game, or go shopping.
- *Relax:* Relax somewhere that makes you feel peaceful, take a walk, go to the woods, daydream, watch a sunset, go to the library, listen to the radio or to the sound of the ocean or a running brook.

The veteran may turn to his or her workbook now. Have him or her write down ONE activity from EACH category that he or she will do this week to help him or herself get better.

Choose one activity from each category above that you might be able to do in the next week.

■ Section E: Common pitfalls

Veterans may have a lot of reasons to not engage in proactive coping behaviors, especially when they are feeling depressed. Here are some common reasons that keep veterans from doing the things that will make them get better. As you review this section with the veteran, use the discussion to help them understand that these are *common* hindrances to positive coping. It is reasonable to expect that veterans will experience one or more of these. However, rather than letting these pitfalls get in the way, they should be anticipated as predictable challenges on the road to better health and coping. With this preparation, veterans will easily see these challenges approaching—encourage them to be prepared to overcome them as they have overcome so many other challenges.

There are several common challenges that people frequently encounter. It is important to recognize and be ready to confront these challenges so that they do not interfere with healthy coping.

Feeling numb

Following a deployment, some veterans report feeling like nothing is fun or enjoyable anymore. Remember that the positive spiral can be a slow process. When you start doing an activity, it is likely to feel sort of flat—not fun or rewarding at first. It may be this way for a while. However, over time, positive activities help boost our mood—this also makes it easer for our motivation to increase, making it easier to do the activities. Even better, the activities become more enjoyable. But it takes time and practice.

Avoidance

Remember from Chapter 1 that people returning from the war zone will often avoid activities and reminders of deployment. They may also avoid doing things that were related to danger in a war zone, but that will not really lead to danger back home. For example, some people may avoid driving, being in crowds, or simply sitting in the middle of a movie theater because it triggers reminders of danger. Because the brain and body adjust to dangerous situations, after stress, it is important to help our bodies learn the difference between what is dangerous and what is merely uncomfortable. The only way to do this is to practice being active again. We have to give ourselves the chance to re-learn that most activities are safe.

Having no motivation

When we are depressed, we are least likely to do the things that we need the most to keep our lives on track. Depression makes it difficult to motivate ourselves to do the things we need to do: clean the house, pay our bills, or play with our children. However, all of these activities make people feel useful, capable, and independent. Making ourselves complete a task (such as running an errand, organizing a project, doing a job well, or learning something new) will actually help prevent the downward spiral of depression.

Injuries

Injuries or chronic pain may keep you from doing the same types of activities that used to be fun or rewarding. *But it is very important not to let that stop you!* Again, when you first start doing an activity, it is likely to not be fun or rewarding at first. It may be this way for a while. Additionally, it may take some time to find new activities. One veteran, for example, was in a wheelchair and was no longer able to play catch with his 10-year-old son, as he used to. Rather than give up the game, this man brought out his 7-year old to help. His younger child caught the ball for him, and then the veteran threw it back to his older son.

Life changes

Changes in life—including relocation—may also keep you from doing the exact types of activities you used to do. Again, it may take some real creativity and problem-solving skill to find new activities that are rewarding for you. For example, a veteran loved to mountain bike. However, she was now stationed somewhere with no mountains. Rather than give up biking, she bought a racing bike and started taking bike tours a few times a week. Although at first she missed mountain biking, over time the new activity replaced mountain biking and became just as much fun.

■ Section F: Putting coping activities in action

WHAT TO DO

- We have talked about a bunch of different ways to control stress. But we need to find some ways that work for each of you personally. That's what we are going to do right now.

- It is important that the veteran attempt(s) to manage stress on a daily basis—not just when he or she is especially stressed out. You will want to explain to them the importance of breaking these activities down into manageable goals. Unless they schedule and plan on doing them, it is only another New Year's resolution on the fridge.

- For example, maybe someone would be willing to commit to lift weights for 30 minutes, two times a week on Mondays and Wednesdays, running or walking two times a week on Tuesdays and Thursdays, meditating for 30 minutes on Friday nights, and swimming for 30 minutes on Saturdays and Sundays. It is important to be specific.

- Have the veteran go to the Goal-Setting section of this chapter of the workbook.

- Take a few minutes to break each stress management activity down into manageable goals for their week. Discuss when the veteran may be able to do each activity they choose during the coming week. In making a commitment to try a new positive coping behavior, it is important that the choice be realistic—help the veteran to find activities that suit them in terms of physical capability, availability, and schedule. There is a section for writing down and scheduling activities in their workbooks. Writing down commitments and following up on them is very important. With no commitment, they are less likely to engage in these activities.

1. Choose one positive coping activity that you want or need to do in the next week.

2. How can you make sure you accomplish this activity? Break the activity down into smaller steps. For example, let's say you have gotten behind in your house cleaning and do not have any motivation to clean. You may set a goal to spend 15 minutes a day this week cleaning your home. One day you can do a load of laundry. The next day you can put all your clothes away. The next you can vacuum the bedroom.

3. Identify which days and times you will complete the activity next to the activity, and write down how long—and how often—you would be willing to do the activity.

A NOTE ABOUT GRIEF

Grief is a normal and natural response to loss, but if neglected it can affect you in ways that you may not notice at first. Because talking about losses and death is often awkward and uncomfortable, veterans suffering from grief often avoid dealing with their thoughts and feelings related to loss. If you are having high levels of grief or guilt, we urge you to talk to your chaplain or a mental health professional.

■ Section G: Treatments for transition stress

As mentioned in Chapter 1, one of the most common treatments for transition stress reactions is cognitive-behavioral treatment with a professional who is trained in dealing with these concerns. If you are bothered by reactions like the ones we have been discussing, it may be useful for you to work with a trained mental health professional on ways to deal with these reactions. It may also be useful to work with a primary care physician or psychiatrist who can prescribe medication to help ease some of the symptoms. Medications can help neurochemicals in the brain to readjust to healthier levels, which can help you to reduce your anxiety as well as help to manage your reactions to things.

▶ When to talk to your doctor

Have you or someone you know been:

- Feeling very depressed and discouraged?
- Using drugs or alcohol more than normal, or using them as an attempt to numb the pain inside, or as the only way to relax or sleep?
- Feeling overwhelmed by your symptoms?
- Thinking of hurting yourself or someone else?

Did the veteran answer YES to ONE or more of these questions? If so, have them talk to their doctor right away.

▶ The heart of the matter

The transition from the war zone will be an ongoing, daily, gradual process. In this section, we provide you with the tools you will need to deal with reactions some people experience following war. We help you begin a plan of action so that you can be better prepared to cope with the transition back into civilian life. Specifically, we encourage you to use several types of activities that promote good feelings and help ward off depression, such as positive body-focused activities, goal-focused activities, and positive social activities. These activities will promote better mood and better overall health. We encourage use of these healthy coping behaviors on a regular basis. Engaging in these healthy coping activities will help promote the upward spiral of recovery.

- Please turn to the end of the chapter and take the quiz. Remember that the quizzes are a good way to review some of the important points in the chapter.

▶ Phone calling exercise

As with the previous chapter, assign the Phone Calling Exercise. If treatment is in a group context, it is useful to provide a question to each veteran to help facilitate their calling and give them a starting point for their call.

1. Complete the Phone Calling Exercise Worksheet in the same way that you did for the last session. Remember to note your SUDS before and after each call.

2. On your own, we would like you to look over the list of healthy coping activities in this chapter. Identify one activity from each of the four categories (body-focused activities, goal-focused activities, social activities, and other positive activities) that you are willing to do in the week ahead. By reviewing these activities and even adding similar activities to these lists, you will eventually be able to select a number of coping activities to participate in to increase your resilience.

3. Use the Coping Activity Schedule at the end of this chapter to write down the days and times that you plan to engage in at least one positive coping activity per day. For example, maybe you would like to choose swimming as an activity. You could write down and schedule yourself to go swimming for 30 minutes, three times per week on Mondays, Wednesdays, and Fridays. Here are two examples of how other veterans planned to participate in coping activities:

Joe Is a Father of Two Who Works as a Project Manager

- For day one, Joe planned to go to his favorite take-out restaurant and have a lunch he really enjoyed.

- He intended to focus on learning a new computer program that he's been meaning to become skilled at, and that he enjoys doing, for 15 minutes each day.

- He planned to spend an hour playing with his kids in the yard when he gets home.

Dennis Is a Single 18-Year-Old Who Works as an Airplane Mechanic

- For his plan, Dennis chose to call a favorite buddy that he used to work with, but who now works in another building, and to say hi during his lunch break.

- Because he enjoys inspecting and caring for planes, he planned to challenge himself at work by seeing how quickly and efficiently he could complete the inspections he was required to do every morning.

- He also planned to rent a comedy dvd Friday night that would get him laughing.

After returning from an experience as profound as war, it can be very difficult to get back into habits that will keep you healthy and help you cope with problems. When too many serious problems are happening, it is hard to remember to take time for yourself. Sometimes we feel we do not have any more energy. But taking time for healthy coping activities is important. It is really important at this time to fight against the urge to "veg out" or to turn to other negative coping habits. It may take some time, and it may not even feel fun at first. Reversing the downward spiral takes extra effort. Making these activities a part of your daily lifestyle is an important first step toward healing.

Phone Calling Exercise Worksheet

Name: _____

Session Number: _____

Question: _____

Person Called	Date	Your Own SUDS Before (0–10)	Answer/Topic	Call Length	Your Own SUDS After (0–10)

▶ Coping activities schedule

We need to develop a plan of action to help us cope with the transition from the war zone. We may not feel interested in the kinds of activities that we used to think were fun. Injuries and chronic pain may make us unable to do the kinds of activities we used to that kept us at our best. Therefore, we have to identify new activities, and make the time to do something fun every day.

Use the Coping Activity Schedule to write down times when you can do a healthy coping activity from ideas in this chapter. Try to make time for at least three activities per day. Put this schedule in a place in your home where you will see it often, such as on your refrigerator or bathroom mirror.

Coping Activities Schedule

	Monday	Tuesday	Wednesday	Thursday	Friday	Saturday	Sunday
0600 hrs.							
0700 hrs.							
0800 hrs.							
0900 hrs.							
1000 hrs.							
1100 hrs.							
1200 hrs.							
1300 hrs.							
1400 hrs.							
1500 hrs.							
1600 hrs.							
1700 hrs.							
1800 hrs.							
1900 hrs.							
2000 hrs.							
2100 hrs.							
2200 hrs.							
Night ↓							

Hayes, S. C. (2005). *Get out of your mind and into your life: The new acceptance and commitment therapy.* New York: New Harbinger.

Martell, C., & Addis, M. (2004). *Overcoming depression one step at a time: The new behavioral activation approach to getting your life back.* New York: New Harbinger.

Name: _____

Date: _____ _____ / _____ _____ / _____ _____

1. Reactive coping strategies are behaviors that we use to prepare ourselves for problems that might occur in the future.

   True or False

2. Social isolation helps protect a person from problems and is a good way to help a person adjust to being back home after a deployment.

   True or False

3. Setting and achieving goals is an important way to improve mood and decrease depression.

   True or False

4. When a person feels anxious in a situation that used to be comfortable, it means that he or she should get out of that situation as quickly as they can, and avoid that situation in the future.

   True or False

5. As soon as we start doing pleasant activities, we should expect that our mood will change completely, and everything will be okay.

   True or False

6. When we experience very few activities we consider to be pleasant or productive, we are more likely feel depressed. Also, when we feel depressed, we don't feel like doing the kinds of activities that are likely to be a source of pleasure. This is known as the:

   a. Complicated bereavement

   b. Sliding depressive cycle

   c. Downward spiral of depression

   d. Resilient coping

CHAPTER FOUR

Improving Sleep

Sleep problems, including difficulties falling or staying asleep and frequent nightmares, are common among individuals returning from combat deployments. Those deployed to war zones can develop poor sleep habits related to their combat stress symptoms—such as feeling the need to stand guard at night rather than to sleep. Veterans may suffer from nightmares and may try to stay awake for fear of having nightmares. In addition, veterans may try to fix their sleep problem with "solutions" that only make the problem worse such as by drinking alcohol or taking lengthy naps.

In this session, we briefly assess the overall range of sleep problems experienced by veterans, and provide an overview of sleep including a description of the stages of sleep. We address the role of sleep stages, circadian rhythms, and sleep homeostasis to describe what happens when the sleep cycle goes awry. Included is a discussion of how post-war symptoms can lead to sleep problems. We then draw from empirically supported interventions in order to develop a plan to help veterans incorporate good sleep habits into their daily lives. Last, we discuss treatment options for sleep and nightmares.

Some of the core symptoms experienced by those who have recently been in combat are sleep problems. Difficulty falling asleep or staying asleep—known as *insomnia*—is one common type of sleep problem. Additionally, people who have been deployed in combat may suffer from nightmares related to their deployment, or may wake up at night feeling terrified. Others may feel the need to stay awake to protect themselves from danger. Additionally, people may have poor sleep habits that contribute to their sleep problems, such as napping too long and too often.

Sleep problems are expected following combat deployment. Feeling on edge, sleeping for short periods of time, and nightmares all contribute to sleep problems. These problems are related to being exposed to stressful situations, and with help should decrease over time.

In this chapter, you will learn about tools to help you sleep better. We begin, however, by reviewing last week's homework and talking more about different kinds of sleep problems that veterans may be experiencing.

▶ Review of homework

Review the Phone Calling Exercise in a similar fashion to the previous session. Unless there have been significant problems with the completion of the Phone Calling

Exercise, it is appropriate to review this in a brief manner—for example, asking the veteran how many calls they made, what their SUDS was at the beginning and the end of the exercise, and what their impression of the exercise was overall.

Check in with veterans regarding the coping activity schedule assigned in the last chapter. Discuss activities they selected and what they noticed regarding their practice of the exercise (e.g., difficulties encountered implementing the exercise, decisions they made about positive activities to practice, overall reductions in SUDS associated with the practice). Briefly discuss strengths and limitations in their practice during the past week.

If some individuals did not complete homework assignments from the previous session, you may choose to focus on factors that interfered with practice and emphasize the importance of daily practice.

Begin the session with a discussion about sleep problems the veterans are experiencing. For example, if treatment is in a group format, several questions are useful:

- You will want to begin the session by getting your participants involved. We suggest asking all those who are suffering from sleep problems to raise their hands:

    —How many of you are suffering from sleep problems?

    —What kinds of sleep problems are you having?

- As sleep problems are named, find out how many people are having the same problem with more specific questions. For example:

    —How many of you are having nightmares?

    —How many are waking up in the middle of the night?

- As the veterans list sleep problems they are experiencing, the clinician can write them down on the board.

If treatment is in an individual context, similar questions can be used:

- *How has your sleep changed?*
- *What kind of sleep problems have you been experiencing following your military experiences?*

You should provide hope that sleep problems can be fixed (Krakow et al., 2001; Murtagh & Greenwood, 1995). Normalize their experience as being expected and *temporary* following exposure to combat:

Sleep problems are somewhat expected following exposure to combat. Feeling on edge, only sleeping for short periods of time, and nightmares all contribute to sleep problems. These problems are related to being exposed to stressful situations. With help, these problems will decrease over time.

We are now going to describe for you the stages of sleep and how they relate to the onset of sleep problems.

■ Section A: Stages of sleep

Scientific research on sleep stages has shown that when we sleep our brain activity changes throughout the night. Electroencephalograms (EEGs) are instruments that measure the level of activity in the brain. EEGs have shown that our brains go through a series of several stages of activity as we sleep. As we enter Stage 1 of sleep, our brain activity begins to slow down. We experience a loss of awareness of time and where we are. As we enter deeper stages of sleep (especially Stages 3 to 4) we see that our brain activity becomes slower and slower. Figure 4.1 represents the stages our brains go through during a period of several hours of sleep. On the left are listed Stages 1 through 4. On the bottom of the graph, you will see the hours of sleep during the night, hours 1 through 8.

Wakefulness: Our brains are very active when we are awake, taking in all of the information we process.

Stage 1: During Stage 1, sleep begins. We begin to lose consciousness; body temperature, breathing, blood pressure, and pulse rates begin to decrease.

Stage 2: During Stage 2, EEG shows that our brain's activity becomes slightly slower, with bursts of rapid waves called *sleep spindles.*

Stage 3: EEG shows that our brains' activity continues to slow during Stage 3, and brain waves becomes larger.

Stage 4: Stage 4 is the deepest stage of sleep, also consisting of still slower brain activity waves. Muscles are very relaxed and eyes are still.

Rapid Eye Movement (REM) *Sleep:* Our brain activity becomes active again during REM sleep, and our eyes move quickly back and forth under our eyelids. Our breathing, pulse, and blood pressure increase and decrease. Eighty percent of dreams and nightmares occur during REM.

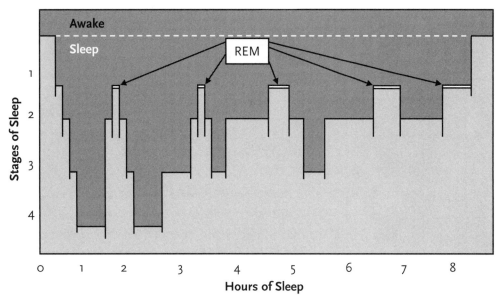

Figure 4.1   Stages of sleep.

The whole process of transitioning through Stages 1 to 4 takes about 90 minutes. Then we transition back up through Stages 4, 3, and 2 for several minutes, followed by a period of REM sleep. People most often have dreams and nightmares during REM sleep. This is why we remember our dreams in detail if we are awakened during REM sleep. REM lasts for only a few minutes until we cycle back into Stage 2. We cycle through these stages several times during the night.

Here are some other important details that sleep research has revealed:

- Scientists find that depriving people of REM sleep, as opposed to other types of sleep, makes people do poorly on learning tasks. It seems that REM sleep—and perhaps dreaming—helps us to learn new material.

- Deep sleep (Stages 3 and 4) seems to help restore the body physically. If we do not obtain the proper amount of deep sleep, then we feel tired and less rested.

- Our bodies have a built-in daily rhythm that is affected by light, darkness, warmth, and physical activity. This is called the light/dark cycle, or the *circadian rhythm.*

This chapter can help you improve habits that will help you get a good night's sleep. But first, let's explore how poor sleep habits can mess up the sleep cycle.

Optional background information

If additional information is desired, it can be useful also to help veterans to understand the systems that help us to regulate sleep. Sleep seems to be regulated by two different systems: circadian rhythms and the sleep homeostat. Although we do not cover these systems in the workbook, you may choose to discuss them in the session. Otherwise go directly to the next section, Sleep Habits and Sleep Problems.

- Circadian rhythms: As part of the body's biological clock, our circadian rhythm is tied to the light/dark cycle by sensors on the retina that deliver the light/dark messages to the brain. For example, a typical cycle includes a period of wakefulness and alertness in the mid evening, after which we become increasingly tired and drowsy. Likewise, if a person tries to stay awake all night, just before dawn they are likely to become very tired, but by 6:00 or 7:00 in the morning, the body naturally begins to become alert again.

  —Manipulating the brain with bright lights in the morning can help the circadian rhythms.

- Sleep homeostat: The sleep homestat is a drive that builds up during the day and is discharged when you sleep.

  —We can encourage sleep by tinkering with the sleep homeostat. For example, we can increase our sleep homeostat by exercising in the morning or by using warm heat in the evening to increase our body temperature.

  —Sleep follows a sharp drop in body temperature, so lying still in bed after a hot bath can help someone drift off to sleep.

■ Section B: How poor sleep habits can lead to sleep problems

- When we experience sleeplessness, a common reaction is to try to sleep more—either by napping the next day or going to bed early the next night. However, doing these things will throw the sleep cycle off.

- Alternatively, a person may drink alcohol to help them sleep. However, as alcohol is processed by the body, it throws off the sleep cycle even more—either causing us to wake up in the middle of the night, or simply reducing the quality of our sleep overall. Either way, the alcohol makes our sleep less restful.

- These attempts to make up for sleep work against the body's natural sleep cycle. This leads to a self-defeating cycle. The more a person tries to make up for lost sleep, the more the cycle is thrown off.

- Eventually, the person begins to become anxious about having to go to sleep. As your brain learns to associate the bed with wakefulness, anxiety, and stress, sleeping becomes an unpleasant activity (Jacobs, 1998).

- Additionally, people who have survived a highly stressful situation—such as war zone deployment—may feel hypervigilant all the time. When people are on guard, the amygdala may be over-reacting, firing up more activity in the nervous system, triggering feelings of stress or danger. This also can interfere with sleep.

- Veterans may have distressing thoughts that pop into their heads when they do not want them to. Focusing on these thoughts will also make it harder to fall asleep. The bedroom environment then becomes connected with the distressing thoughts. And when distressing thoughts are linked to the bedroom, then the bedroom itself becomes a trigger for distress.

- Nightmares and night terrors are also common in people who have gone through highly stressful events. Because nightmares can be very terrifying, after having them often, a person can start to become afraid of lying in his or her own bed or going to sleep at night. The bedroom environment then becomes linked with the fear, making it even harder to sleep.

Many of the tactics people usually resort to as an attempt to get more sleep undermine the body's natural cycle. Such tactics can lead to depression and irritability. On the other hand, good sleep habits work with the sleep cycle to restore restful sleep habits. The next section outlines good sleep habits, which we have broken down into activities taking place at nighttime, morning, and daytime. As you read the good sleep habits, think about changes you can make to your own sleep.

■ Section C: Good sleep habits

Using an interactive style, discuss with the veteran(s) an overall pattern of good sleep habits. Prompt them to think about changes they can make to their own lives in order to improve their sleep.

List on a board or page three titles: Nighttime, Morning, and Day. Now we are going to explore the types of sleep habits that have been shown to help promote good sleep. As we discuss the different habits, think about what changes you might be able to make in your life. After we talk about the different techniques that can help to improve sleep, I am going to ask you to come up with three different new habits you are willing to implement in the week ahead.

Nighttime

Activities that will help promote sleep in the evening involve slowing down physical and mental activities. Helping the body prepare for sleep include warming the body a little and relaxing the muscles. Darkness and quiet will also help tell the brain that it is time to sleep. Specific activities that are good nighttime sleep habits include:

Winding down

It is important to wind down both physically and mentally in the hour before bedtime by engaging in relaxing activities such as light reading, a calming hobby, doing relaxation exercises, or listening to relaxing music.

- During the wind-down period, avoid stimulating activities such as phone calls, arguments, work, paying bills, playing action videos, or watching TV shows.

Sleep rituals

A sleep ritual is a nightly habit or relaxing activity to help promote sleep. Sleep experts recommend that people with sleep problems spend 30 minutes to an hour prior to sleeping doing a regular activity that will ready the body and mind for sleep.

- When this activity is performed nightly for at least three weeks, it will become a habit that helps to promote sleep. Some suggestions are to:
  —Drink a warm glass of milk or decaffeinated tea.
  —Listen to relaxing music.
  —Take a warm bath or shower.
  —Read a light and even boring book or magazine.
  —Light a candle and pray.
  —Do a simple crossword puzzle or other enjoyable puzzles.
  —Do some deep breathing or another relaxation technique to calm the body and mind.

It is important to remind veterans that sleep rituals should involve calming activities that help to prepare the mind and body for sleep. Even watching television, reading novels, working on difficult puzzles, can in some cases be more engaging, stressful, or excitatory. For example, some individuals frequently keep a television on and watch a variety of programs just before trying to sleep. Watching the news, action movies, or other programs with noncalming themes interfere with, rather than promote, sleep.

Sleep medication

Some medications for sleep, such as Valium, are addictive and will make sleep even more difficult over time:

- Newer sleep medicines assist with strengthening the circadian rhythms, and generally do not interfere with the REM stage of sleep or one's ability to dream. Yet, there is still the possibility of physical and emotional dependence on a medicine, so they should be used with caution and only as temporary solutions.
- Antidepressants, on the other hand, can help sleep by strengthening the sleep stages and the sleep/wake cycle.
- Prescribed and over-the-counter medications should be taken as indicated by one's doctor, and should be accompanied by good sleep habits.

Bedroom environment

It is important to make your bedroom a safe, peaceful environment. Here are some suggestions of how you can do this:

- Make your bedroom comfortably dim or dark.
- Make your bed comfortable.
- Block out noises with a white noise generator, air purifier, or fan.
- Keep your bedroom temperature comfortable.
- It may help to add peaceful and comforting images to your bedroom, such as poems, prayers, or pictures of your children, pet, or a religious figure.

Keep bedroom only for sleep and sex

Your bedroom should be used for only two purposes—sleep and sex. Here are some more suggestions to help you get better sleep:

- Use the bedroom for sleep and sexual activity only.
- Do not try to go to sleep when you are not drowsy. Instead, engage in a sleep ritual until you become tired.
- If you want to go to sleep but do not fall asleep within 30 minutes, do not lie in bed tossing and turning. Instead, go to another room and engage in a quiet relaxing activity—such as reading a magazine or a book—until you feel drowsy.

Do not try to make up for lost sleep

Going to bed early in order to catch up on sleep seems like a good idea, but the more time you spend in bed (if you are not sleeping), the more you mess up the sleep cycle.

- Try to go to bed at the same time each night and get up the same time each morning, even if you do not sleep well.

Some nighttime sleep habits I can change to improve my sleep include: _____

_____

_____

Morning

Activities that will improve wakefulness in the morning are those that stimulate the mind and the body. Bright lights and activity will help tell the brain that it is time to wake up. Specific good morning habits include:

Regular rising time

- Trying to catch up on lost sleep can actually hurt your ability to sleep.
- Do not sleep late after a bad night of sleep. The extra sleep in the morning will actually interfere with your sleep the following evening. Keep a regular time to get up every morning, even if you do not have to go to work.
- Instead of sleeping in late, plan an enjoyable activity in the morning such as reading the newspaper or taking a walk to help make waking up early more pleasant.

Increasing sun exposure

- One thing we can all benefit from is exposure to sunlight. Sunlight is an important timing cue for waking, and so it is helpful to be exposed to sunlight early in the day (of course, wear sunscreen as necessary).
- Even on a cloudy day, the light from the sun is much stronger than indoor lighting.
- Light from the sun improves mood and energy and will help the natural sleep cycle.

Morning sleep habits I can change to improve my sleep include: _____

_____

_____

Daytime

There are also things we can do during the day to strengthen the sleep/wake cycle.

Napping

- Taking long naps can be detrimental to you getting a good night's rest, although many cultures have naps as part of their daily routine.

- A nap as short as 10 minutes can improve mood, alertness, and mental performance. However, long naps or naps late in the day can interfere with the sleep cycle.

- Limit your nap to no more than 30 minutes and do not nap later than 4 PM.

Increasing exercise

- Not getting enough exercise can keep you from sleeping.

- Lack of physical activity can contribute to insomnia by causing a flattening of your body temperature rhythm.

- Exercise can improve sleep by causing your body temperature rhythm to rise and fall during the day.

- Exercise can also help sleep by improving your overall energy and mood.

Decreasing caffeine

- Drinking beverages containing caffeine, even during the daytime hours can hurt your chances of getting sleep.

- Similar to alcohol and other drugs, caffeine can disrupt the sleep cycle, causing sleep to be less restful. Coffee, tea, some drinks, and chocolate all have high levels of caffeine, so they should be avoided in the afternoon and evening.

Decreasing alcohol

- It is true that drinking alcohol can help people fall asleep, however, the sleep will last for only a few hours until alcohol begins to be metabolized. Then the withdrawal from alcohol will cause mid-night awakenings or reduced sleep quality. Alcohol also tends to interfere with the REM cycle and one's ability to dream. All of these changes decrease sleep, and make it less restful.

Decreasing smoking

- If you smoke near bedtime or after waking during the night, the stimulant effect of nicotine (or withdrawal) may keep you awake—or may interfere with the sleep cycle—resulting in less restful sleep.

Decreasing stress

- Events and situations in life can cause us to have sleep problems.

- Sleep problems often begin in response to a stressful life event. It is important to perform stress-reducing activities to help you sleep better (see Chapter 2).

A daytime habit I can change to improve my sleep is: _____

_____

_____

■ Section D: Nightmares and night terrors

After being in-country, veterans may experience at least a few nightmares or night terrors:

- During *night terrors,* people wake up terrified but cannot remember a dream.
- During *nightmares,* people may feel as though they are reliving the event, or may feel the same fear, helplessness, or rage that may have been experienced during their war experience.

Night terrors and nightmares are not a sign that you are going crazy. Rather, they are your mind's way of processing a stressful experience. Some veterans try to avoid nightmares, by using drugs or alcohol, or by avoiding sleep altogether. These attempted solutions only lead to new problems, such as substance dependence and sleep deprivation. This also usually results in more irritability and depression, poorer memory, and increased stress and anxiety.

Coping strategies for nightmares and night terrors

We suggest the following for coping with nightmares or night terrors:

- If you are confused or anxious after waking from a nightmare or night terror, it is helpful to "ground" yourself by shifting your focus to the room around you. Look around (if there is enough light to see) and begin labeling the objects you see in the room. For example, say to yourself or out loud: "That is my desk. Those are my clothes. This is my bed. I am in my room. That is my partner next to me." until you are less confused.
- It is helpful to get up and go to another room to get your bearings. If you still feel confused or anxious, "ground" yourself by focusing on and labeling the objects in that room. It may take a while to reorient yourself to where you are and the present time.
- It is helpful to write the nightmare down. Doing this can make the dream less real and help you calm down faster. It can also be a good way to begin to share the dream with someone close to you, which can help you begin to have control over the nightmare.
- After you feel reoriented to the present, practice your sleep ritual.
- If possible, reach out to someone you feel safe with—who supports you. If you live with others, find time to talk to them about the fact that you are having nightmares. Discuss ways in which you both might want to handle the situation.
- A small percentage of sufferers act out their nightmares in their sleep. You may want to rearrange your bedroom so that you are safe. If you share your bed with a partner, you may need to make sure he or she is not in harm's way.
- If your nightmares do not decrease over time, know that there are effective treatments available (Davis & Wright, 2007; Krystal & Davidson, 2007).

■ Section E: Treatment for sleep problems

There are effective treatments for sleep problems. However, choosing the one that is right for you will depend upon your situation. If your sleep problems do not go away with time, contact a mental health provider who has expertise in sleep disorders and PTSD. Therapy that addresses the way you think and act (called cognitive behavioral therapy) can help bring about long-term relief of sleep problems. Cognitive behavioral therapy for sleep disorders targets your beliefs and behaviors that can make sleep problems worse. Specific therapy and medications for nightmares can also be very helpful in improving sleep and other stress reactions. Breathing and relaxation therapies also may be used to help reduce muscle tension and promote sleep.

Additionally, many antidepressants can help improve sleep and strengthen the sleep/wake cycle and sleep stages. For example, antidepressants such as Wellbutrin, Prozac, Paxil, and Celexa may actually help restore the natural sleep cycle. Of course, sleep medications are available for quick, short-term relief of insomnia and nightmares. But some sleep medications can be addictive and may have side effects, so check with your doctor to find out which treatment is best for you.

▶ When to talk to your doctor

Have you or someone you know been:

- Having difficulty falling or staying asleep several times a week?
- Having repeated nightmares or night terrors?
- Repeatedly waking up screaming, crying, or feeling panicked, but not knowing why?
- Feeling so overwhelmed that you might hurt yourself or someone else?

Did the veteran respond YES to ONE or more of these questions? If so, have them talk to their doctor right away.

▶ The heart of the matter

Some of the core symptoms experienced by those who have returned from war are sleep problems—such as insomnia and nightmares. Additionally, individuals often have poor sleep habits that contribute to their sleep problems, such as napping too frequently or too long, or keeping an irregular sleep schedule. Some veterans suffering from post-deployment reactions may also try to fix their problem with "solutions" that only make the problem worse (e.g., using alcohol or other drugs, or by sleeping all day). Good sleep habits involve working with the body's natural sleep cycles so you can sleep better.

- Please turn to the end of the chapter and take the quiz. Remember that the quizzes are a good way to review some of the important points in the chapter.
- Please note that helpful resources and references on insomnia are provided for you in the reference section in the back of this book.
- Please take a few minutes to complete the brief quiz at the end of this chapter. It wll help you remember what you have learned in this chapter.

1. Complete the Phone Calling Exercise Worksheet in the same way that you did for the last session. Remember to note your SUDS before and after each call.

2. Identify three new sleep habits you are willing to try every day for the next three weeks:

   1. _____

   2. _____

   3. _____

3. Use the Sleep Habit Schedule on the next page to write down the days and times that you plan to practice your new sleep habits. You may want to schedule more. Perhaps you may want to choose one type of activity from each category for each day.

In addition to completing the Sleep Habits Schedule provided in the workbook, veterans can also choose to add their new behaviors to the Coping Schedule they started in Chapter 3. Suggest that they post the schedule in a prominent place they see often (their bathroom mirror or their nightstand) to remind them to engage in the new behavior.

Phone Calling Exercise Worksheet

Name: _____

Session Number: _____

Question: _____

Person Called	Date	Your Own SUDS Before (0–10)	Answer/Topic	Call Length	Your Own SUDS After (0–10)

Sleep Habits Schedule

Use this schedule to write down the days and times that you plan to practice your new sleep habits. Keep the schedule somewhere where you will see it daily.

	Monday	Tuesday	Wednesday	Thursday	Friday	Saturday	Sunday
0600 hrs.							
0700 hrs.							
0800 hrs.							
0900 hrs.							
1000 hrs.							
1100 hrs.							
1200 hrs.							
1300 hrs.							
1400 hrs.							
1500 hrs.							
1600 hrs.							
1700 hrs.							
1800 hrs.							
1900 hrs.							
2000 hrs.							
2100 hrs.							
2200 hrs.							
Night ↓							

▶ Further readings for the clinician

Davis, J. L., & Wright, D. C. (2007). Randomized clinical trial for treatment of chronic nightmares in trauma-exposed adults. *Journal of Traumatic Stress, 20*(2), 123–133.

Jacobs, G. D. (1998). *Say good night to insomnia.* New York: Henry Holt.

Krystal, A. D., & Davidson, J. R. T. (2007). The use of Prazosin for the treatment of trauma nightmares and sleep disturbance in combat veterans with Post-Traumatic Stress Disorder. *Biological Psychiatry, 61*(8), 925–927.

Sharp, T. J. (2001). *The good sleep guide: Ten steps to better sleep and how to break the worry cycle.* Berkeley, CA: North Atlantic.

Name: _____

Date: _____ _____ / _____ _____ / _____ _____

1. We have dreams every night that we sleep.
   True or False

2. Sleeping in late is a good way to catch up on lost sleep.
   True or False

3. Alcohol and certain medications (such as Valium, Xanax, and over-the-counter sleep medications) can mess up our sleep cycle.
   True or False

4. Antidepressants can mess up our sleep cycle.
   True or False

5. Taking a 60-minute nap can mess up the sleep cycle.
   True or False

6. If you cannot fall asleep at night, it is best to perform a stressful, highly demanding task that will tire you out and help you fall asleep.
   True or False

7. If you wake up and cannot get back to sleep, it's best to get out of bed (even in the middle of the night) and engage in a light, somewhat boring, activity.
   True or False

8. One way to cope with a nightmare is to write it down.
   True or False

Dealing with Anger

People with post-deployment stress reactions often feel irritated or angry, which can lead some of them to act impulsively when triggered by conflict. Because they may feel on edge, veterans suffering from a stress reaction are at risk for getting into various altercations. The purpose of this chapter is to help veterans become more aware of, and better understand, their anger so that they:

- Are better able to identify when they are becoming angry
- Understand the link between their adaptive reactions to war, and their current hyperarousal, irritability, or anger
- Understand that anger can be channeled into healthy or unhealthy activities
- Are better able to manage anger without aggression and other impulsive behavior.

People returning from long deployments often feel irritable and angry. Because some veterans may feel on edge, they are at risk for getting into trouble—be it with their spouse or partner, coworkers, supervisors, strangers, or the law. To prevent problems associated with high irritability and anger, it is important to become aware of cues that can let you know when you when these feelings are increasing. The purpose of this chapter is to raise awareness of your irritability and anger so that you are better able to identify them and prevent problems from taking place. We also discuss how anger can be channeled in either healthy or unhealthy ways. We conclude the chapter with a basic technique to help you reduce the chance that your anger will get you in trouble.

▶ Review of homework

Briefly review the Phone Calling Exercise, asking the veteran how many calls they made, what their SUDS was at the beginning and the end of the exercise, and what their impression of the exercise was overall.

Check in with the veterans regarding specific sleep habits they chose to improve, new sleep habits they chose to practice, and their completion of the Sleep Habits Schedule. Discuss changes that they found to be helpful, as well as challenges to implementing changes.

If some individuals did not begin practicing good sleep habits, or did not experience benefits, you may choose to focus on factors that interfered with practice, as well as emphasizing the importance of daily effort in changing habits. Also, remember that change takes time, that consistency is very important, and that it may take time for sleep quality to improve even with consistent improvements in habits.

▶ Combat and anger

Begin by helping veterans understand the relationship between war and increases in feelings of irritability and anger. Discuss with veterans that while anger is helpful in-country, it can be hard to turn off after returning stateside. Key points include:

- Increased irritability may be related to overall over-activation of the amygdala, and increases in overall levels of anxiety and fear. As such, these feelings of irritability and anger may be related to successful adaptation to the war environment. Long-term exposure to a combat environment (i.e., adaptation to being constantly on guard for danger) can sometimes increase levels of anger.

- Those who were in actual combat also may have grown accustomed to tapping into their anger to give themselves the motivation and energy to accomplish their missions successfully; anger is an emotion that facilitates aggressive action, which is adaptive in a combat environment.

Veterans learned how to adapt to the war zone, where sudden bursts of anger enabled them to spring into action. Anger may have given them the energy to stay alive. In this chapter, we help them to stop or prevent this cycle by empathizing with their symptoms, letting them know that they alone are responsible for their actions, and helping them to develop tools to manage anger reactions. In the next section we help veterans become aware of anger and see how feelings of irritation and anger can be harmful. This exploration should help them develop a basic understanding of what happens physically when one gets angry. We then explore anger outlets that are healthy and productive mentally and behaviorally. Furthermore, we explore whether anger is good or bad.

It is also important for veterans to understand that reducing their overall level of irritability and anger is one part of their overall readjustment following their deployment. As they do all of the different exercises in this program, and work in numerous ways to help their system adjust to being back in a safer environment, many changes will begin to take place. Among these are improvement in sleep, feeling more at ease in generally safe environments, feeling less edgy, and feeling less irritability and anger overall.

■ Section A: What is anger?

You may begin introducing the topic of anger by asking the veterans what they think anger is. As they share their thoughts, you can list their ideas on the board or on a sheet of paper. Beginning with these questions gets veterans engaged and helps them to begin thinking about anger more flexibly:

- What is anger? Are there different kinds of anger?

Allow the veteran to share his or her thoughts. The veteran can generate his or her own list of words associated with anger and different types of anger—such as annoyance, frustration, disappointment, irritation, hurt, and rage.

Add other words to their list as necessary to round out the concepts with words they may not have come up with themselves. Introduce the concept of anger as energy that can be focused for use in either harmful activity or for use in helpful, productive activity. Veterans can be reminded that they may be feeling extra irritation and edginess right now, and may need to take extra steps to take care of themselves. Although anger is a common and expected reaction, the impact of anger over time can be extremely damaging.

Next, discuss the physical ramifications of anger—that is, the physiological changes that occur when one becomes angry. Provide a brief basic layman's description of what happens physically and chemically inside the body during anger, and explore the mental changes that take place.

The veterans may go to the workbook and list feelings they have when they get angry. Help them to understand these feelings as signs or cues that they are getting angry. Recognizing these signs is a critical step toward beginning to manage anger.

Anger is a feeling we have when the world is not going the way we want. What happens to the body when a person becomes angry?

- Muscles become contracted and tense
- Heart pumps faster
- Breathing becomes quicker
- Stomach tightens
- Body feels hot

When we get angry, adrenaline and other chemicals pour into the bloodstream to shift the body into high gear, generating energy for action.

What happens mentally when we get angry?

When we become very angry, it really interferes with our thinking. When adrenaline and other chemicals in the body become overly charged, the logical part of the brain gets tuned off, and our behavior becomes more impulsive, illogical, and desperate. The angrier we are, the more foolish we get.

What are some feelings, sensations, or thoughts *you* have when you get angry?

■ Section B: Risks and benefits from anger

Risks of anger

After introducing the concept of anger, find out whether veterans understand that anger is not bad per se:

- Is anger good or bad?

Guide the veteran to a fuller understanding of the risks of unmanaged anger, as well as the benefits of modulating and utilizing anger effectively. If treatment is being conducted in a group context, allow for a free-flowing discussion—letting veterans share their ideas about the risks and benefits of anger. In individual treatment, it may be useful to use a more Socratic method in discussing the same issue. In either case, using Socratic questions is helpful in leading to the conclusion:

■ Anger is not bad or good—it all depends on how you use it.

It can be powerful to describe some recent examples where impulsive anger led to some dire consequence. You may include a discussion of what type of healthy behavior choices could have been made in the situation to have prevented the harm.

How can anger be hurtful?

Anger can lead to a slew of problems, such as:

■ Poor thinking and decision making
■ Ruined relationships
■ Divorce
■ Work problems
■ Lost promotions
■ Dismissal from jobs
■ Arguments or fights
■ Spousal abuse
■ Legal and financial problems
■ Incarceration
■ Health problems (e.g., headaches, heart disease, high cholesterol, immune system disorders, chronic pain, stomach disorders, diarrhea, and early death)

Benefits of anger

Discuss with the veteran the potential benefits of anger:

■ With so many risks that go with anger, should we try to stop feeling angry? Are there also benefits? What are some of the ways that anger helps you?

After a list of points is generated, summarize it for them and build in a conclusion:

■ So it all depends when and how anger is expressed. It's important to know how to recognize anger and express it appropriately.

Remember to keep a focus on the importance of keeping the whole system—the brain and body—calmed down enough that we can still make effective choices. While some anger can provide a boost in energy that can increase effectiveness, letting it go too far is much more likely to interfere with good reasoning and a focus on our actual goals. Another way to say this is that letting anger go too far makes us much less effective.

Should we try to stop feeling angry?

No! As long as we are alive we will have reasons to be angry from time to time. Some levels of anger and conflict are inescapable in relationships. Therefore, we need to learn resilient ways to cope with anger, and to keep it from being too frequent or too intense.

What is healthy anger?

Anger that is expressed in helpful ways is healthy anger. When we are able to react to situations with logic, we can be angry without letting the feeling get us in trouble. Additionally, we can channel the energy we get from anger in healthy ways to help motivate ourselves, and help us achieve what we want.

How can anger help us?

- Anger can help people reach their goals.
- Anger can give people energy.
- Anger can motivate people to work harder.
- Anger can help people solve problems.
- Anger can help people handle emergencies.

List some healthy ways that you can channel your anger: _____

_____

_____

■ Section C: How can I prevent harmful anger?

It is very important to take some time to step back from a situation that is triggering feelings of anger. It is important to be able to think logically so that you identify a healthy way to handle the feeling.

There are three important steps to prevent harmful anger:

1. Notice when your stress or anger level is increasing.
2. Build in a pause or take a time-out.
3. Identify healthy ways to resolve anger.

Step 1: Notice when your stress or anger level is increasing

The first step is to pay attention to your level of anger, just as it is important to get a feel for the level of stress you may be experiencing. An anger scale, similar to the SUDS stress rating scale, can be a helpful guide in this respect (see Figure 5.1).

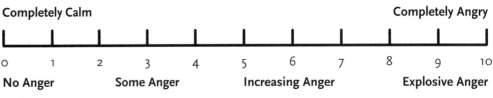

Figure 5.1 Anger scale.

- As discussed in a previous section, it is important to keep your stress level below 5. Similarly, when anger rises above 5, it is a cue to use relaxation methods or some other healthy coping behavior to restore your ability to think. Remember that when your level of irritation and anger are already high—when you are "running hot"—even something small can bump you up higher to where you are more likely to react badly. Keeping your overall level of irritation lower and noticing your anger climbing earlier gives you more time to catch it when your anger starts getting higher.

- Practice tuning in to your own cues that help you to know when you are getting angry. Remember that these cues might be:
  - —Changes in your body, such as butterflies or tension in your stomach, beginning to sweat, feeling your heartbeat get faster, tension in your arms or chest, etc.
  - —Other sensations in your body, such as feeling dizzy or lightheaded, a headache, or nausea.
  - —Specific repetitive thoughts, such as "I cannot believe we are having this same argument *again*—every week it's the same thing," "they are doing this on purpose to make me mad," or "I will teach them not to mess with me," or things that we tell ourselves when we are getting upset (and which also make us *more* upset).

What are some cues that tell you when you are becoming angry?
Where is your anger level right now? _____ / 10

Step 2: Build in a pause or take a time-out

Once people understand how to monitor their anger, they can take additional steps to stop themselves from acting out in ways that could harm themselves or others. When they find themselves in a situation where they are feeling very angry, they must resist acting impulsively—instead they can distract themselves or remove themselves from the situation so that they can calm down. It is important to calm down and think clearly before acting.

The easiest way to calm down is to build a pause in between the feeling of anger and your reaction to it—this is commonly referred to as a time-out (Edleson & Tolman, 1992; Paymar, 1993; Pence & Paymar, 1993; Rosenbaum & Leisring, 2001). Some people are able to calm down by counting to ten. Some people can think of a person who is calming to them, a particular scene (such as a lake), or some other relaxing image (such as the color blue) that will distract them from the issue that is getting them riled. It is important to practice and find the time-out method that works best for you.

Discuss the rationale for using a time-out, based on being able to recognize one's own signs of anger escalating, and stepping away from the situation that is triggering feelings of anger (Rosenbaum & Leisring, 2001).

Emphasize the idea that the time-out period is to be used to calm down so as to be able to better handle the situation—it should not be used as a way to permanently avoid problems, or control the relationship by shutting down the other person. Rather, it is a way to interrupt one's own escalation of anger. During a time-out, we take a break and use positive, healthy behaviors to help ourselves calm down, so that we are better able to handle stressful situations without acting in a threatening or aggressive way (Edleson & Tolman, 1992).

What is a time-out?

A time-out is a technique for people who sometimes get into trouble because of acting impulsively, or who react too quickly or too extremely because of anger. The purpose of the time-out is to provide you with an opportunity to step back from the situation that is making you angry. Stepping back, and temporarily removing yourself from the situation, gives you time to cool off, think about things, and make better choices. Time-outs are described more at the end of this chapter (see the handout on pages 90–91 of this chapter called Time-out).

If you are in a long-term relationship and have problems with anger, we suggest talking about time-outs with your spouse or partner. Have a preplanned signal that lets your spouse or partner know that the situation is getting out of hand and a cool-down period is needed. For instance, in one couple either party would hold up their hand in a halt posture and say, "I am taking a time-out." The other party would then step back and allow their spouse or partner an hour to cool down. It is important to plan for these situations ahead of time to make the time-out effective.

Here are some important questions to think about and answer for yourself:

- Who can I use time-outs with?
- What are some situations that a time-out can help with?
- When do I know that I need to use a time-out? What are the cues to look for that tell me I am becoming angry—physically, emotionally, or otherwise?
- What can I use as my preplanned signals?
- Where can I go during a time-out to cool off?
- What are some ways that I can calm down when I am becoming very angry?

Step 3: Identify healthy ways to resolve anger

Once you cool down, you can think about healthy ways to deal with your feelings. When you are calmer, it is easier to explore your options so you can better understand the actual cause of the anger, and make a logical decision about what you are going to do.

The cause of the anger may or may not be obvious. For example, you may be yelling at your spouse or partner for burning dinner, but you are really angry with a coworker for snubbing you earlier in the day. You may want to explode at someone in line at the store, but really you know you are irritated because you slept poorly the night before.

If there is a conflict that you are angry about, you can then take positive steps to resolve the problem, rather than letting the angry feelings linger. It often is important to talk to others (for example a friend, family member, therapist, or pastor) who are not part of the conflict, about your problem.

What are some healthy things that *you* can do to help resolve your anger?

■ Section D: Treatments for anger

If you have noticed your anger level has been peaking a lot lately, and have a hard time controlling it, please know there is help. One very important part of treatments for anger is in helping a person to identify the specific cues that relate to their anger. There are anger management workshops people can take to learn more about managing anger reactions and practice more ways of calming down. There are also medications that can be helpful for people who have trouble controlling their anger.

▶ When to talk to your doctor

Have you or someone you know been:

- Making poor decisions that have been hurting you or someone you care about?
- Having a lot of conflicts with your boss, supervisor, or coworkers? Or are you having legal problems or trouble holding a job?
- Having trouble communicating with and getting along with your spouse or significant other?
- Feeling so overwhelmed that you might hurt yourself or someone else?

Did the veteran answer YES to ONE or more of these questions? If so, have them talk to their doctor right away.

In closing, it may be important to acknowledge that veterans have served for months on end during which they sacrificed their own well-being for our safety. A lot of veterans report feeling on edge, easily frustrated, and quick to anger. They may have had to adhere to strict limits to what they could do in their role because of the huge task involved. They may feel responsible for things that were not in their control.

Some will feel as though their efforts were meaningless, and so will need to be redirected to the broader significance of their role. The closing discussion for this chapter can be geared to any specific situations the group may have encountered in-country or may be encountering now. Remind veterans that they alone are responsible for their behavior, and acting impulsively can result in paying dire consequences that sometimes cannot be reversed. There are more resilient ways to see the world. Remind them that there are helpful steps they can take to deal with angry feelings:

■ Unfortunately, this world is not always fair. When we focus on injustices, we can find a lot to be angry about. This can be especially true after returning from war. You may have just returned from months on end during which you sacrificed your own well-being for this nation's safety. While in a combat zone, you may have had to adhere to strict limits to what you could do to protect yourself or you may have had almost no rules at all. Either way, adjusting to being back may be difficult and may involve a certain kind of culture shock. Because of events that happened during your deployment, you may feel responsible or angry for things that were not in your control.

■ Please remember that it will take time to transition from the war zone. The high level of energy that you may have used to keep yourself alive is no longer needed, but it will take awhile for your body to learn that. In the meantime, it is important to take extra steps so that you do not do something you regret.

■ You alone are responsible for what you do. When you channel your anger in healthy ways, you can use anger to achieve what you want.

▶ The heart of the matter

A lot of veterans report feeling on edge, easily frustrated, and quick to anger. You may have just returned from months on end during which you sacrificed your own well-being for this nation's safety, or you may have been back for some time. You may have had to adhere to strict limits to what you could do to protect yourself. You may feel responsible or angry for things that were not in your control. Please remember that it will take time to transition from the war zone, and that it also takes skilled practice and effort to help our system adjust to being back. The high level of energy that you may have used to keep yourself alive is no longer needed, but it will take awhile for your body to learn that. In the meantime, it is important to take extra steps so that you do not do something you regret. When you channel your anger in healthy ways, you can use anger to achieve what you want.

■ Please turn to the end of the chapter and take the quiz. Remember that the quizzes are a good way to review some of the important points in the chapter.

All of the new habits that the veteran is developing—coping behaviors, sleep habits, and stress management techniques—will help them to manage their anger. Remind the veteran that it takes time to change habits and to continue to practice these behaviors they have been working on in the week ahead.

▶ Phone calling exercise

As with the previous chapter, assign the Phone Calling Exercise. If treatment is in a group context, it is possible that by this point in the program, the veterans may not need to be given a question for the phone calling exercise, and can be asked either to make up their own question to ask, or simply to make the phone calls and speak to the other veterans. Even if a question is not given, make sure to continue emphasizing the importance of making the phone calls.

▶ On your own

1. Complete the Phone Calling Exercise. Remember to note your SUDS before and after each call. Complete details about this exercise are included in the On Your Own section at the end of Chapter 1.

2. Identify a possible future situation where you may have to deal with your anger:

   ■ What are the cues to look for—physically, emotionally, or otherwise—that will let you know that you are becoming angry?

   ■ What are some healthy things that you can do to help resolve the situation?

3. Practice using the time-out technique. Plan ahead, by thinking about the type of situations in which you might need a time-out, and how you will implement it.

▶ Time-out

This is a useful technique for people who have trouble managing anger productively and instead sometimes react to anger by acting out in unhealthy ways.[*] The purpose of a time-out is to provide you with an opportunity to step back from the situation that is making you angry, and to think about your options before you make a decision about what you are going to do. In order to be successful, you must practice this technique consistently. If you have a partner, review these guidelines with him or her, so that you can agree on how to use the time-out technique, and so that each of you will know what to expect.

1. *Monitor:* When you are having an argument, or in other situations that you anticipate may be upsetting to you, closely monitor your SUDS and your level of anger.

2. *Notify:* When you notice yourself getting angry to a such a level that think you may act in a dangerous or hurtful way, say out loud to yourself and the person

---

[*] Adapted from Edleson & Tolman, 1992; Paymar, 1993; Pence & Paymar, 1993.

with whom you are angry: "I'm beginning to feel really angry, and I need to take a time-out."

3. *Explain:* Tell the other person where you are going and when you will return. Usually one hour is a reasonable amount of time—enough to cool down, but not so much that you are simply avoiding the issues.

4. *Positive action:* During the time-out, choose a positive place and activity to help calm yourself down and begin improving the situation. During this time do *not* use alcohol or drugs, and avoid driving. It is best to do something healthy that will help you to get your anger out, such as going for a walk, exercising, doing a noncompetitive and nonviolent hobby or sport, or talking to a positive person who can help you to calm down. This can be a great time to call someone else in the group for support. You may also use relaxation skills, such as muscle relaxation, deep breathing, and relaxing imagery. During this time, take a mental time-out and do not allow your thoughts to escalate your anger.

5. *Coming back:* Return on time, based on the amount of time you said you would be away. Call your partner if you are coming back earlier or later than you said, so that they also have had enough time to cool down, are not surprised, or waiting for you.

6. *Offer to talk:* When you return, ask the other person if he or she would like to talk with you. If you both want to discuss the situation, tell the other person why you think you became angry. You may also want to talk about what it was like for you to take a time-out. If you feel yourself again wanting to explode, take another time-out.

7. *Respect his or her desires:* If the other person does not want to talk, do not force it. Respect the other person's need not to discuss it at this time. Some topics of conversation are too "charged" to talk about right away or without a helper. Put the issue on the shelf for a while, accepting that it is too difficult for the two of you to discuss it alone. Even if it is an important issue, *remember that your first priority is to prevent violence.*

Time-outs can be hard to do. Why? Because some of us are taught to believe that only a coward will walk away from a fight. Your impulse will be to stay and finish it, or at least to get in the last word. You may feel your self-respect is on the line. Even worse, you may feel very afraid when you walk away. Consider these "hot thoughts" as your enemies, not your protectors. Remember, an argument does *not* mean that your life is in danger, and in a relationship violence will *not* get you what you want. Practicing this new skill is part of stopping the cycle of destructiveness, anger, and depression, and taking a step towards more effective coping.

Finally, like learning any new skill, taking a time-out may be difficult at first. Many people tend to give up quickly after initial failure. Remember you have to unlearn many years of destructive behavior and learn something new. It will not happen quickly. It will not happen perfectly the first time, or even the second. However, with conscious commitment and practice, taking time-outs will become easier in time.

Phone Calling Exercise Worksheet

Name: _____

Session Number: _____

Question: _____

Person Called	Date	Your Own SUDS Before (0–10)	Answer/Topic	Call Length	Your Own SUDS After (0–10)

► **Further readings for the clinician**

Reilly, P. M., & Shopshire, M. S. (2002). *Anger management for substance abuse and mental health clients: A cognitive behavioral therapy manual* (DHHS Pub. No. SMA 023661). Rockville, MD: Center for Substance Abuse Treatment, Substance Abuse and Mental Health Services Administration.

Name: _____

Date: _____ _____ / _____ _____ / _____ _____

1. Being angry for long period of time may lead to:
   a. High blood pressure
   b. Early death
   c. Stomach disorders
   d. All of the above

2. Which of the following is an **unhelpful** thing to do when you get very angry?
   a. Count to 10
   b. Take a time out
   c. Try to argue your point
   d. All of the above

3. Which of the following is a **helpful** use of your anger?
   a. Use anger to help you work harder
   b. Use anger to help motivate you to reach a goal
   c. Use anger to help you solve a problem
   d. All of the above

4. If your anger level is 5 or over (on a scale from 1 to 10) you should perform a healthy coping behavior.
   True or False

5. Returnees coming home from the war zone tend to be very calm and relaxed.
   True or False

6. Anger is a "bad" emotion that can only lead to conflict and aggression.
   True or False

7. List 3 cues that tell people when they are becoming angry:

   _____

   _____

   _____

CHAPTER SIX

Reintegrating with Society

In this session, we address common reactions veterans can have that may make the transition into civilian life more challenging. We explore and describe various strategies to assist veterans as they reintegrate back into society. We also provide ways that veterans can continue to utilize positive coping strategies during the adjustment phase.

FACTORS INCREASING REINTEGRATION STRESS IN VETERANS

There are a number of factors that modulate how stressful the experience will be for veterans returning from a deployment. It is important to realize that not only was the war experience stressful for the veteran, but their stress will also be increased by the reaction of their family and friends, and that of the broader society. As an individual and as part of society, the veteran has numerous issues to deal with. Here are some of the factors that will relate to increased stress in the veteran during this transition period:

- More dangerous duties in war
- Others in their military unit being seriously injured or killed
- More exposure to seriously wounded or dead people
- Exposure to or threat of exposure to toxic chemical warfare or other weapons of mass destruction
- History of past traumas
- Increased, unexpected time overseas in a war zone (e.g., having a deployment extended)
- Loss of vocation or livelihood
- Reduced income and financial stressors
- Children feeling abandoned and having negative reactions toward veteran-parent
- Being overburdened by new roles and responsibilities
- Being faced with new relationships and changes since they have been gone
- Non-ideal family environment after returning, compared to how they thought it would be
- Being second-guessed by family for decisions they made while away to war
- Disrupted, previously-established patterns or routines
- Not knowing how to communicate with spouse, partner, or significant others

Even veterans who are very resilient may react to this transition with a period of increased distress. It is expected for them to experience days or weeks of mild to moderate symptoms of depression, anxiety, and anger.

- *Normal* is an individualized process, meaning that each veteran may respond differently to this period.

- How a veteran reacts reflects his or her own coping style. Some temporary negative responses during this period are expected because each person has a unique history.

- Those with more complicated histories, such as past traumas, may react more intensely in some way.

▶ Review of homework

Briefly review the Phone Calling Exercise, asking veterans how many calls they made, what their SUDS was at the beginning and the end of the exercise, and what was their impression of the exercise was overall. Review their plans to manage anger in specific situations that they identified as high risk in the previous session.

Check in with veterans regarding their ongoing practice of techniques to manage their own anger, including awareness of their own cues and anger signals, healthy behaviors focused on helping resolve situations, and practice of the time-out technique. Briefly discuss strengths and limitations in their practice during the past week.

If some individuals did not practice coping strategies since the last session, you may choose to focus on factors that interfered with practice, as well as emphasize the importance of daily practice.

You may be having some really mixed feelings about your time at war and about your return to the United States. Maybe you thought that the transition would be easy, but you are finding out that is not completely true. In this session, we discuss common difficulties that many veterans face as they adjust back to civilian life.

▶ Reintegration

Going from the foxhole to your front porch is a profound change to make in a short amount of time. Sometimes you may feel like you are still fighting the war. It takes time to adapt back to civilian life, and you may still find yourself acting in ways you never have before. When you get in tighter spaces or crowds, you may feel trapped or in danger. You may still feel on guard, even at times when logic says that things really are safe. It is possible that you may be overwhelmed by noise and confusion, even in your home. You could be on a totally different schedule for sleeping and eating than your family.

What are your biggest concerns as you transition back into civilian society?

- Veterans may write down their biggest concerns by answering the question provided in their workbook. Help them to break those problems and obstacles down into manageable, obtainable goals that can be worked on over time.

- Have the veterans briefly describe his or her experiences in coming back. This is a chance for them to share their experience in a supportive and safe environment. In the case of group treatment, this is also an opportunity for veterans to unite on their experiences. It helps them know they are not alone in feeling the way they do.

- Discuss the return from deployment, and encourage the veteran to solve his or her problems with positive solutions. Becoming avoidant, passive, or helpless only fosters more helplessness, which can lead to depression. Help empower the veterans by exploring positive solutions to his or her problems.

  —Are these the best ways to deal with these problems? If not, what are some other options?

In this next section, we will also discuss some common pitfalls and difficult areas, and positive ways of dealing with their physical and emotional pain.

■ Section A: Major reintegration issue—Control

Going through really difficult and painful experiences during war deployments can leave people with a feeling of being out of control. Many people feel like they cannot control what is going on in their environment or in their lives. In fact, there are many things in our lives that we simply do *not* have the power to control. For example, you may not have control over parts of your life because you are in the military. Here are some examples of things you may not have control over:

- Where you are stationed
- When you will be deployed
- How long you stay on deployment
- How other people behave
- Crowds at a grocery store
- The weather
- Unwanted memories and other combat stress reactions

What types of things do you feel you do not have control over right now?

- Discuss with veterans some of the things that they still feel that they cannot control right now.

- Normalize the feeling of often wanting to control all areas of life, and recognize the reality that the vast majority of outcomes are influenced by numerous factors, typically placing outcomes beyond our control.

- Focus also on things over which we do have control—many internal factors, and the contribution we make to numerous situations. However, there are plenty of things in life we can control. For example:

  —We can control what we do in our free time.

  —We can control who we spend our time with.

  —We can control how we treat other people.

  —We can control out attitudes about life.

  —We can control our choices about our future.

Name some things that you *do* have control over right now.

It is important to recognize the things in life that we *can* control, and those things that are *not* in our control. When we put our focus and efforts on things within our control, we are able to be more effective and more successful.

■ Section B: Major reintegration issue—Hypervigilance

Vigilant people are alert to danger in the environment. In a war zone, maintaining a high level of vigilance is extremely useful. Being on constant alert for danger is critical in keeping yourself alive because you never know which person or what item might be deadly on the street. In the war zone, staying highly alert becomes second nature.

Over time, however, people in a war zone often get used to feeling threatened—in their environment or with other people—and they may continue to feel that way when they return home. When people return from war, it is common for them to be *hypervigilant,* overly alert for possible dangers. They may be hypervigilant because they overestimate the possibility of danger.

Hypervigilance is not useful in a safe environment. In fact, as we discussed in earlier chapters, long-term hypervigilance can be dangerous—it interferes with sleep, contributes to excess levels of stress and anger, and actually makes people *less* likely to detect real danger, and less capable of dealing with actual dangerous situations.

It is possible that you have been overestimating danger as well. Your friends or family members may make comments that you look tense, or you may be avoiding activities that you used to enjoy. These feelings are expected for those returning from war. It may take time to adjust to being with other people or in unknown environments.

There are a number of ways that you can overcome hypervigilance. Initially, your body and brain have to be retrained to accept that many situations may feel uncomfortable, even when they are not dangerous. For example, you may feel uncomfortable being around lots of people—such as being in a crowd or going to the mall. To begin getting used to doing some of the things you enjoyed in the past, gradually practice being around other people. You may want to start with small groups. Also, starting off in places you are familiar with will help you adjust back to the fact that you are no longer in danger.

When you begin spending more time in environments that might trigger reminders of the war zone, remember to monitor to your stress cues and SUDS, and use your tools—belly breathing, progressive muscle relaxation, grounding—as you practice tolerating the environment. With practice, you can slowly recondition yourself to feel comfortable in situations you used to enjoy—and even begin to enjoy them again.

Some tools that I can use to cope with hypervigilance include:

_____

_____

_____

Have veterans who have felt hypervigilant discuss how they have been coping with it.

Are these the best ways to deal with their problems? If not, what are some better options?

It is important that you help yourself begin to feel more in control and as safe as possible. If you are doing healthy things to take care of yourself, bravo! You have crossed a bridge. You are on your way to healing. *Good for you!*

■ Section C: Major reintegration issue—Coping with civilians

Coming back to the United States and into civilian society can be very stressful. After being away in a foreign country, in a battle zone, escaping death, or facing death every day, coming to everyday life can be a huge culture shock.

- Everyday life can seem mundane, trivial, and almost like a betrayal when there are still warriors left behind.

- Veterans may have lost their jobs, their wives or husbands, or their livelihood. They may have missed weddings, funerals, or major milestones in their children's lives.

- Veterans may have to deal with antiwar comments and insensitive questions from civilians.

Veterans will have numerous opportunities to implement the skills they learned in the previous chapters.

Expect a culture shock for a while as you adjust back to life in the United States. You have spent time in a foreign country, perhaps in a battle zone among the enemy and routinely facing possible death or injury. After returning from the war zone, everyday life can seem boring. It may feel like not being at war is betraying the friends you left behind. You may feel angry because civilians are not paying attention to what the military is doing. You will run into people who have strong opinions about the war. Some are okay with it—and some are not. And some will ask very stupid and insensitive questions.

A good way to deal with the return to civilian life is to think about the types of problems you might run into and how you might deal with them. Thinking ahead about common problems veterans face, and how you might handle them, can head off problems before they begin.

As an example, you may want to think ahead about healthy ways to handle people who provoke you. Consider the following:

- What would you do if someone made an offensive statement to you? How would you handle it if it were different people?
    —A friend
    —Someone you work with
    —Close family member
    —A stranger

Use the question above to lead a discussion among veterans—that someone makes an anti-war statement to them. How would they handle it?

▶ Hold on! Did you need a time-out?

In the anger chapter, we talked about time-outs. To repeat, time-outs are great because they defuse the situation. It's like breaking up two boxers and putting them back in their own corners of the boxing ring. It gives people a few minutes to think about things, to sort things out. After returning from the war zone, it may be harder to keep your cool and it may take extra time to chill out.

- You may want to go back to the anger section and review what you learned about healthy ways to manage and reduce anger.

Reintegration plan exercise

We cannot change other people or past events. But when we examine ourselves, we find that we do have control over many of the choices in our lives. It is extremely important for us to recognize when we *do* and *do not* have control, so that we can take care of ourselves. It is important for you to be able to answer these questions:

- What things or people trigger my anger or stress reactions? What sets me off?
- How do I deal with anger or other feelings when I am triggered?
- Are the ways I am dealing with this bad for me? If so, what can I start doing differently? (be specific)

BARRIERS TO COMMUNICATION

One very important thing that needs to take place to make things better is for veterans to become aware of their thoughts, feelings, and reactions that can impact communication with other people.

Have the veteran list communication problems he or she has been having, and help them come up with effective communication for these situations. Although this section is not in the workbook, you may wish to have veterans take a few minutes to discuss the questions below:

- Do you tend to isolate yourself from other people? If so, let's talk about the reasons for doing so and possible consequences of this.
- Do you believe that no one else can possibly understand what you are going through? What would you like people to understand about you, or about what you have been through?
- Are you able to feel all kinds of emotions—happy, sad, angry, joyful, empathy? If not, what has changed for you?
- How do your friends feel about your coming back? What is your impression?

  —You have gone through a lot. You went to fight a war. That is a *huge* stress. Then you came back. A lot of veterans think they should be happy all of the time because they are back with their families, and they feel guilty that they do not feel like that. Maybe you feel that way, too.

■ Section D: Treatments for reintegration difficulties

We have talked about how there are a lot of different areas in your life that have changed since you got back home. An area that requires adjusting is being able to deal with hypervigilance and hyperarousal. Another is getting used to crowds. It might be difficult and challenging to talk with civilians now. Other people may not understand what is going on, or may not care. If any of these continue to be difficult for you, please know there is help available.

Treatments for reintegration stress will vary depending on what your main concerns are now. But no one needs to suffer alone. Treatments and counselors are available to help you through this time.

Ask the veterans to continue to do the Reintegration Plan exercise after today's session. This will help them plan ahead to use their good communication and time-out skills in the week ahead. This will also help them to come up with good ways of dealing with triggers in their environment.

▶ When to talk to your doctor

Have you or someone you know been:

- Feeling trapped, suffocated, closed in, or panicky when you are in tight-spaced areas or in crowds?
- Feeling angry at or disconnected from others, or like no one can understand what you are going through?
- Feeling overwhelmed by your reactions?
- Thinking you might hurt yourself or someone else?

Did the veteran answer YES to ONE or more of these questions? If so, have them talk to their doctor right away.

▶ The heart of the matter

In this chapter, you learned that the reactions that you may be having right now are common for service members who have come back from a war. This is an adjustment process for you. As a warrior, you have so much strength and courage inside of you. If you doubt this for even a second, please remember you did what most people never do—you survived deployment! You survived then, and you have what it takes to keep on surviving.

- Please turn to the end of the chapter and take the quiz. Remember that the quizzes are a good way to review some of the important points in the chapter.

▶ Phone calling exercise

As with the previous chapter, assign the Phone Calling Exercise. If treatment is in a group context, it is possible that by this point in the program the veterans may not need to be given a question for the phone calling exercise and can be asked either to make up their own question to ask, or simply to make the phone calls and speak to the other veterans. Even if a question is not given, make sure to continue emphasizing the importance of making the phone calls.

▶ On your own

1. Complete the Phone Calling Exercise. Remember to note your SUDS before and after each call. Complete details about this exercise are included in the On Your Own section at the end of Chapter 1.
2. Do the Reintegration Plan exercise in this chapter to plan what you will do to cope with people who trigger anger or stress. Continue to practice good communication and time-out skills with others. Keep using your new skills, and you will find that things go more smoothly when there are problems.

Phone Calling Exercise Worksheet

Name: _____

Session Number: _____

Question: _____

Person Called	Date	Your Own SUDS Before (0–10)	Answer/Topic	Call Length	Your Own SUDS After (0–10)

▶ **Further readings for the clinician**

Armstrong, K., Best, S., & Domenici, P. (2006). *Courage after fire: Coping strategies for troops returning from Iraq and Afghanistan and their families*. Berkeley, CA: Ulysses.

Name: _____

Date: _____ _____ / _____ _____ / _____ _____

1. People who are hypervigilant:
    a. Always help other people who are in need
    b. Think they are sick even when they are well
    c. Are overly alert for danger even when danger is not present
    d. All of the above

2. We can control every aspect of our environment and our life.
    True or False

3. "Thinking ahead" is an important part of making healthy decisions and reintegrating with society.
    True or False

4. What are some situations or people that trigger stress reactions for you?

    _____

    _____

    _____

5. What healthy coping behaviors can I use to deal with the people and/or situations that trigger stress reactions?

    _____

    _____

    _____

◀ CHAPTER SEVEN ▶

Reintegrating with Family and Friends

For veterans who get sent back home after being in a war zone, there may be some very mixed feelings about being reunited with their families and other loved ones. Most of them feel relieved to be getting into a safer living zone. Still, many veterans may also feel conflicted because they feel like the people they deployed with are the only ones who can understand them.

As previously mentioned, it is common for those returning from a war to get irritated more easily and to isolate from others due to feelings of discomfort. It is possible that the veteran may experience numbing of affect, and he or she may find it hard to have feelings such as love, happiness, empathy, and sadness.

Veterans may also be experiencing some underlying anger or resentment from the spouse or partner, as well as the children in the family, for leaving them. Family members may be experiencing a multitude of problems themselves, including worry and fear for the safety of their family member while he or she was away at war. These feelings are expected after the relief of having him or her at home. Sometimes such emotions are difficult to make sense of, and may be expressed as anger at loved ones.

All of these issues can present some problems in communication between the veterans and their significant others. In this chapter, we address difficulties veterans can have reintegrating with their family and friends, and provide methods that can help them readjust more easily.

When warriors return from deployment, the number one thing they talk about is how they now feel different. It is true! You have changed and you are different. And those around you have changed, too. Time changes everyone. Maybe you feel happy to be back in the United States and with people you love, or maybe you do not. Often warriors have grown used to being in the war zone and wish they were "back there." You may be dealing with practical problems. For example, you may be returning to family problems that you had before you left, and are not feeling happy about having to deal with them again. In this chapter, we describe strategies that can help you deal with these problems so you can reintegrate back with your family and friends.

▶ Review of homework

Briefly review the Phone Calling Exercise, asking the veterans how many calls they made, what their SUDS where at the beginning and the end of the exercise, and what their impression of the exercise was overall.

Also briefly review the Reintegration Plan exercise they filled out last week.

Check in with the veteran regarding their ongoing practice of good communication and time-out skills with others. Briefly discuss strengths and limitations in their practice during the past week.

If a veteran did not practice coping strategies since the last session, you may choose to focus on factors that interfered with practice, as well as emphasizing the importance of daily practice.

▶ The important role of families and friends

Often, the primary source of support for the veteran is his or her spouse or partner, parents, grandparents, children, siblings, and other extended family members or close friends. For many war veterans over the years, family and friends have been extremely important in helping them deal with and overcome transition stress. This is because families and friendships provide:

- Companionship
- A sense of belonging
- Self-esteem that can help prevent depression and guilt
- Opportunities to make a positive contribution by helping others
- Practical support
- Emotional support to help in coping with life stressors

Families and friends play an important role in helping you connect with other people. If you are having a rough time reconnecting with those you used to be close with, you may be feeling very frustrated. You may also be wondering if things will ever get back to normal.

■ Section A: Connecting with your family and friends

Not everyone is able to make the transition back to family life with ease. You have changed. Your family and friends have changed as well while you were gone. It is possible that you have wondered if you still fit into your family. It will take time for everyone to get used to each other again. You may be feeling different and even acting different. Because of this, your behavior can affect others in your life.

Below are some changes that other veterans have experienced. Have you noticed any of these in your own life?

- Some veterans have felt a loss of interest in activities. This can confuse family and friends and make them feel cut off or left out.
- Some veterans have difficulty trusting and feeling close to others. As a result, family and friends may feel hurt and betrayed.

- Some veterans may feel like they need to be in control at all times and not show emotions besides anger, which can hurt their relationships.
- Some veterans may be reluctant to talk about what happened in the war zone, which might make family or friends feel left out or insignificant.

How are the problems you are having right now affecting those close to you?

Highlight that what the veteran is feeling and experiencing is expected.

"You have gone through a lot. You went to fight a war. That is a huge stress. Then you came back."

"You may be getting messages that you should be happy all of the time because you are back with your family. You may feel guilty that you do not feel totally happy. If you do, that's okay."

■ Section B: Special issues for couples and children

Veterans often report changes in their relationships with their spouse or partner following deployment. Problems commonly come up that can make getting back together as a couple very challenging and difficult.

Here are some typical problems that you may face as you transition back to being a couple:

- Face-to-face communication may be hard.
- Sexual closeness may be awkward, or it may be difficult to connect like you used to.
- Because of stress you may have lost interest in sexual activities, which may lead to your spouse or partner feeling hurt.
- You may feel closer to your military buddies, and feel like your spouse or partner is a stranger.
- The roles you all used to play for basic household chores may have changed.
- Your spouse or partner may be more independent now, or he or she may have learned new coping skills.
- You may have changed in your outlook and priorities in life. Or, maybe your spouse or partner's priorities have changed while you were away.

Similarly, returning parents sometimes face common problems related to their children. Here are some typical problems that you may face as you transition back to being a parent:

- Your children have grown and may be different in many ways.
- Your children may not remember you, or may be slow to hug you or communicate with you.

- If you have younger children, they can sometimes become clingy or act younger than their age because of the adjustment.
- If you have older children, it is possible that they may be acting indifferent, as if they do not care about you.

Are any of these true of your experience? What problems are you having with your spouse, partner or children right now?

It is a very common expectation for veterans and their significant others to believe that once they return to the United States they will transition back into home and society life easily and that the change will be a smooth one. Unfortunately, this is sometimes far from the case.

Please know that it is expected for your family life to be affected after coming back from war. You may wonder if it can ever be okay again. A lot of veterans think they should be happy all of the time because they are back with their families, and they feel guilty that they do not feel that way. Maybe you feel that way, too. We have found that there are some rules of thumb that can help people readjust to family life again. We will discuss these in the next section.

■ Section C: Suggestions for reintegration

Here are some suggestions to help you as you transition back with your family and friends:

- Take time to listen to your spouse or partner, children, and other important family members and friends. Make individual time for each person.
- Take time, such as a whole day away, for just you and your spouse or partner to renew your relationship.
- Go slowly when reestablishing your place in the family. Roles may have changed and will need to be renegotiated.
- You might need to take some breaks by yourself or with your buddies, for yourself. Or, your spouse or partner may need some breaks at times because he or she is not used to having you there all of the time. It will be an adjustment for both of you, as well as your children.
- Make efforts to explain to your family and friends what you are feeling and what you would like or need from them. It is very helpful to communicate any changes to your family so that they understand why you may be different. Remember that family members may need help understanding how you have changed.
- Keep in mind that your experience was and *is* very different from that of your family. Be patient and remember that it will take some time for all of you to readjust back to normal life.
- Share with your family some stories about your deployment. You do not have to share everything—just what feels comfortable for both you and your listener.

This can provide you with some more emotional support, and help your family to know that they are important enough that you feel comfortable in sharing a part of you with them. It can help all of you heal and bridge the gap that formed while you were away.

- Support and reinforce good things your family has done while you were gone.
- Be prepared to make some adjustments. A family is not a military unit. You may have to renegotiate with them regarding family responsibilities and routines.

Returning home is difficult to do when things are not going as planned. It may be important to cut yourself and your family some slack. Remember that it takes time to get used to being back—be patient with yourself and your family. You all need to get used to each other, as you currently are.

■ Section D: Dealing with the change

So, the question that you may be asking yourself is: My problems are much bigger than this, what do I do to make it better? Well, first off, we cannot control everything that happens outside of ourselves. What is more important is *how we control ourselves*.

You *do* have control over how you deal with all of this. And that is *very* important to remember.

Communicating with others, maybe slowly at first, will help to solve these problems. But every one of us needs support from people in our lives. Bucking up and playing it strong all the time will only make it harder for you and your family to heal. Other people can give you perspective and ideas about how to tackle a problem. If opening up to your friends and family is difficult for you now, here are three steps to help guide you:

1. First, remember that it is common to be having difficulties and a lot of mixed emotions right now. It is expected to feel frustrated at times. Solving problems with others will involve balancing other people's needs with your own.

2. Second, remember that healthy relationships are associated with lower levels of depression. Examples of healthy relationships are those in which a person feels:

    - Liked,
    - Respected,
    - Understood,
    - Appreciated, and
    - Accepted (Lewinsohn, Hoberman, Teri, & Hautziner, 1985).

    Identify people in your life who make you feel like this. These people are those you feel comfortable talking with and who are probably better able to help you.

In the following space, list people you would feel okay talking with or asking for help. This can be your friends, family members, coworkers, boss, chaplain, or a therapist. Try to think of people from different areas of your life (e.g., not all service members, or not all family members). If you do not have people in your life who you feel respect and accept you, think about others—chaplains, therapists, or other professionals who can listen to you. If you have more than five people, great. This is just a start:

1. _____
2. _____
3. _____
4. _____
5. _____

3. Last, actually *talk* with people you feel comfortable with about the problems you are having. Identify at least one person from the previous list who you will talk to about problems reintegrating in the week ahead.

■ Section E: Fighting fair

What if talking with others is not working? What if you are having a problem with a friend or family member? What if you are very angry with them? One of the things that can make it hardest to talk to people close to us—like a spouse or romantic partner—is arguments. When disagreements come up it is important to be able to resolve issues. In other words, it is important to "strike while the iron is hot." This means, do not stuff your feelings in or expect your family and friends to know what is bothering you. Express your feelings when you are upset in a calm and civilized manner. Bottling in your anger will only create further tension, which will lead to resentment and dysfunction in your relationships.

Some people believe that arguing in a relationship is harmful. In fact, all relationships require two people to be able to disagree, and to be able to figure out how to get through it together. However, it is also important to be able to discuss problems in a way that *builds up* the relationship, instead of breaking it down. A number of experts have discussed effective ways of improving communication and building better relationships (Beck, 1988; Gottman & Silver, 1999; Guerney, 1977; Jacobson & Christensen, 1996). Following the advice of these experts, we can learn how to discuss, and even argue, in a way that helps instead of hurts. We can learn how to *fight fair*! Here are some rules for fighting fair:

Rules for fighting fair

Plan ahead

Rather than waiting for an argument to start with someone, schedule time to discuss a problem. Let the person know that you want to work toward a solution during this time, and agree on a time to talk about it. This will give both of you time to think about the important issue, and to approach the discussion calmly, with no surprises. Choose a time when you can talk without interruptions and distractions to bring up problems before they get too big.

Keep your eyes on the prize

In an argument, if the goal is to "win at any cost," then the relationship will suffer. However, if we want things to go better in the relationship, then we need to focus on a different goal—reaching a resolution that is peaceful and satisfying for both of us.

Focus on yourself by using "I" statements

When you bring up an issue, talk about yourself by starting off with the word "I." Tell the other person how you feel, and what you think about the issue. Making accusations is not going to help resolve the problem. When we start using "you" statements (such as "You make me angry" or "You never help me" or "You always . . .") the other person is likely to feel blamed and become defensive. Instead it is better to start off with "I" by making statements such as, "I *feel* angry when you turn the TV sound up high" or "I *feel* frustrated when you let the kids fight with each other."

Stick to one topic

Bring up a *specific* issue that has recently occurred. Tell the other person exactly what happened, and why it bothered you. Avoid using the words "always" or "all the time." For example, instead of saying "You nag me all the time!" say "I feel angry when you tell me not to watch TV, because I need a break sometimes."

Resist the urge to bring up other topics or other past incidents. Don't make the discussion a time to list everything the other person has ever done wrong. Keep focused on resolving the issue at hand.

Stay Calm

When we become too "jacked up" and upset, we are not likely to think clearly, and we are more likely to say and do things that just will not help the situation. You have learned a lot of skills you can use to help yourself to stay calm—put them into practice here. It may be important to take breaks during the discussion, so that you and your partner can use skills to stay calm. Use these breaks as a way to calm down—not to make yourself angrier, or to keep thinking about what you want to say next. This will also make it more likely that you can continue to use all of these rules for fighting fair.

No "below the belt" shots

Name-calling, foul language, threats, and sarcasm will make arguments worse. Each of these distracts from the main point. They will destroy an argument, rather than helping to find common ground, and can destroy a relationship. A common saying from recovery programs puts it this way: "Say what you mean, mean what you say, but don't say it mean."

If you are having a hard time thinking of what to say to your family or friends, use the Communication Plan Exercise to help you get prepared.

Review the rules for fighting fair with the veteran. Help him or her to understand each of the points, and draw examples from the veteran of how each can be used. In many cases, it may be important to address the anger that underlies many stumbling blocks to good communication.

Below are some key points to keep in mind when discussing this concept:

- Plan ahead: Agreeing on a time that is acceptable to both partners is part of treating each other fairly, removing the surprise or "sneak attack" factor from arguing, and beginning to work together. It is also a great way to avoid arguing at certain times that will predictably make things worse (e.g., arguing late at night when both are tired, arguing when either or both individuals have been drinking alcohol, arguing first thing in the morning before work). This also means not avoiding arguments, giving the silent treatment, or sulking. Refusing to fight has been described as one of the dirtiest forms of fighting.

- Keep your eyes on the prize: Some individuals at times view the goal of arguments as needing to win—and they are more likely then to use destructive and coercive methods to win the argument. Discuss the value and importance of these relationship preserving and relationship-building techniques for keeping the relationship healthy, and for reducing overall stress. Remember that while an unhealthy relationship is likely to be a source of much stress, a healthy relationship can be a source of great comfort and healing.

- Use "I" statements: Issues are more likely to get resolved if people accept responsibility for their role in the issue, rather than placing all of the blame on their partner. Saying "I feel frustrated when you do not help me" is much less threatening then "You never help." Also, some people may be tempted to use false "I" statements, or false feeling statements. For example, rather than being a legitimate "I" statement, saying, "I feel like you are a jerk," is actually: (a) expressing a thought, not a feeling; (b) a "you" statement; and (c) a simple insult. Emphasize being honest about one's own "I" statements, focusing on one's own feelings, and accepting responsibility for one's own choices.

- Stick to one topic: It is easy to become overwhelmed (and start thinking and acting less reasonably) if trying to solve every problem at once. One specific problem at a time is enough.

- Stay calm: Use of time-outs may be important. However, time-outs should not be used to control the other person. Staying calm during a disagreement is an excellent way to express to one's partner concern and respect. It is a way to convey to them that: "I care enough about you to listen to what you say, and take what you say seriously even if my view is different."

- No "below the belt" shots: Shouting, name-calling, foul language, threats, and sarcasm are all classic ways of sabotaging communication. There are also other ways that couples may push each other's buttons. Any time that we know we will be upsetting the other person, or undermining healthy communication, we are taking "below the belt" shots.

■ Section F: Communication plan exercise

Review the Communication Plan Exercise with the veterans. Remember that two of the factors that may be interfering most with veterans' relationships at this point may be anger and their desire to isolate from and avoid others.

As you discuss the topic of communication, and expressing one's needs to others, remember that in many situations individuals may be inclined to present their needs in a manner that is overtly angry or frustrated. Help the veteran to explore and understand the problems associated with this approach (including, for example, that when we shout, people are often *less* likely to understand what we are saying, and more likely to register only the anger and discomfort of the situation). Also, discuss more positive ways of conveying one's wants and needs, in a way that makes it more likely that the other person may want to help.

Many veterans may have a strong urge to avoid social contacts; however, as we discussedin Chapters 1 and 2, when veterans give in to this desire they also reduce the opportunity for positive and healing experiences. Thus, in addition to managing anger and frustration (as well as other reactions that may sabotage relationships and make them less rewarding), it is critical to practice communication skills that will help produce more positive relationships. Even though it may feel strange to practice communication skills at first, with practice these skills can help to improve relationships.

There are four basic steps in communicating: (1) identify the problem, (2) decide what you want or need, (3) state the message, and (4) get feedback from the person. You need all four steps to have a two-way conversation. Practice these skills again and again to better deal with problems in your relationships with people:

1. *Identify the problem* that you want to resolve with a friend or someone you love.

2. *What* are you trying to tell the person? (What do you want or need? How can you state what you want using an I statement?)

3. What can you say to this person so he or she will not misunderstand you or become defensive? What exactly is bothering you? Be specific. (What is your *message*?)

4. Get *feedback* from the person. (Can the person provide you with what you want or need? How does the other person see the problem? What does the other person want or need?)

Knowing what your needs are, and sharing those needs with others in your life, will help you have rewarding relationships. Hopefully, communicating with others will go smoothly for you. If these new skills do not work for you, counselors are available who can provide coaching on how to begin solving relationship problems.

■ Section G: Treatments for relationship difficulties

Family and friends can be sources of support, but they can also be sources of stress if problems are not worked out. If you continue to have difficultly being with or talking with your loved ones, help is available. Treatments for relationship difficulties are available that can help you during this time of adjustment. Family and couples therapy can help veterans work out their problems with their loved ones in constructive ways. It helps to have a professional who can be objective and who does not take sides. Family and couples therapy helps give people different ways of looking at things, and helps them adjust during difficult times.

▶ When to talk to your doctor

Have you or someone you know been:

- Yelling at your spouse, partner, or other family members a lot lately? Having conflicts that you cannot resolve?
- Feeling disconnected from others, or like no one can understand what you are going through?
- Feeling overwhelmed by your reactions?
- Thinking you might hurt yourself or someone else?

Did the veteran(s) answer YES to ONE or more of these questions? If so, have them talk to their doctor right away.

▶ The heart of the matter

Many veterans feel very different when they return from a deployment. In fact, many things have changed, both for the veteran and for their families. It takes time to feel comfortable with other people again, and it may also take a while to figure out how to function as a family again. It is important to take time to address specific problems that may be occurring during reintegration with family and friends, including practicing good communication with people who are important to you. Remember to be patient both with yourself and with others.

- Please turn to the end of the chapter and take the quiz. Remember that the quizzes are a good way to review some of the important points in the chapter.

▶ Phone calling exercise

As with the previous chapter, assign the Phone Calling Exercise. If treatment is in a group context, it is possible that by this point in the program the veterans may not need to be given a question for the Phone Calling Exercise and can be asked either to make up their own question to ask, or simply to make the phone calls and speak to the other veterans. Even if a question is not given, make sure to continue emphasizing the importance of making the phone calls.

▶ On your own

1. Complete the Phone Calling Exercise. Remember to note your SUDS before and after the calls. Complete details about this exercise are included in the "On Your Own" section at the end of Chapter 1.

2. Your Communication Plan Exercise is your master plan for dealing with conflicts. If you are ready, go ahead and bring up any problem(s) you identified with your family members or friends. You can copy this exercise, or answer these questions in your head when you run into problems with anyone. Use this exercise to help you in having conversation with someone this week.

Phone Calling Exercise Worksheet

Name: _____

Session Number: _____

Question: _____

Person Called	Date	Your Own SUDS Before (0–10)	Answer/Topic	Call Length	Your Own SUDS After (0–10)

▶ **Further readings for the clinician**

Beck, A. T. (1988). *Love is never enough*. New York: Harper & Row.

Fincham, F. D., Fernandes, L. O. L., & Humphreys, K. (1993). *Communicating in relationships: A guide for couples and professionals*. Champaign, IL: Research Press.

Gottman, J. M., & Silver, N. (1999). *The seven principles for making marriage work*. New York: Three Rivers Press.

Jacobson, N. S., & Christensen, A. (1996). *Acceptance and change in couple therapy: A therapist's guide to transforming relationships*. New York: Norton.

Name: _____

Date: _____ _____ / _____ _____ / _____ _____

1. Veterans should be able to adjust back to family life easily and immediately after returning from the war zone.

    True or False

2. Which of the following statements is an example of fighting fair?

    a. I feel angry when you tell me not to watch TV because I need time to relax.

    b. You always nag me when I watch TV.

    c. You wouldn't bother me if you loved me.

    d. I feel like you are always nagging me.

3. Which of the following is a common change returnees may experience that may make it more difficult to reintegrate with the family:

    a. Loss of interest in activities that used to be enjoyable

    b. Difficulty trusting and feeling close to others

    c. Feeling a need to be in control at all times

    d. Not showing emotions besides anger

    e. Reluctant to talk about what happened in the war zone

    f. All of the above

4. Name 3 particular problems that frequently make reuniting as a couple, or with children, more difficult after deployment:

    _____

    _____

    _____

5. Name 4 things that may help with the transition back to being with family and friends (for example, making individual time to spend with each child or important family member):

    _____

    _____

    _____

    _____

Staying Strong

In Chapters 6 and 7, we talked about issues related to reintegration with family and society. Given all of the stress and distress veterans may be experiencing right now, we believe it is extremely important to focus also on some of the positive factors that can come from deployment. Each veteran survived a war. That, in itself, is a tremendous accomplishment and something that they will always have. It is vital that they realize the value in this, and that they come to a place of acknowledging the inherent strength, courage, and fortitude that they have within themselves. It is with these characteristics that they will be able to press forward in the months and years ahead.

In this chapter, we explore the veteran's strengths and values through a series of questions. We also discuss positive growth that occurred as a result of veteran's war experiences. This topic may be difficult for some. Those who are suffering from depression or bereavement, for example, may have particular difficulty focusing on positive aspects of their lives and war experiences. We ask the clinician to use his or her judgment in using this chapter for those who are early in their recovery process. In some cases, the veteran may need to undergo grief counseling before moving on to positive aspects of their experiences. On the other hand, it is important to remember that it is a natural human inclination to avoid difficult and uncomfortable topics. The veteran may be inclined to try to forget many of their experiences, or to recall only the negative aspects. Throughout this program, the veteran has focused on directly addressing problems and has had numerous opportunities to experience positive changes stemming from this direct, non-avoidant approach. Build on these experiences while guiding the veteran through this section, helping them to recognize that in addition to the negative experiences encountered during their deployment, positive elements can be identified as well. Even amidst the highly stressful and even traumatic events, they may find that in some ways they have grown and improved as a result.

As human beings, we all have within us an extraordinary ability to grow from our challenges and hard times. In this chapter, we will explore how hardship can help us grow and discover great possibilities in our lives.

▶ Review of homework

Briefly review the Phone Calling Exercise, asking veterans how many calls they made, what their SUDS where at the beginning and the end of the exercise, and what their impression of the exercise was overall.

Also briefly review with veterans the Communication Plan Exercise they filled out to plan for dealing with conflicts.

Check in with veterans regarding their practice of addressing specific problems (with family members or friends) that they identified, as well as ongoing use of good communication and time-out skills. Briefly discuss strengths and limitations in their practice since the last session.

If some individuals did not practice coping strategies since the last session, you may choose to focus on factors that interfered with practice, as well as emphasizing the importance of daily practice.

▶ Building strength

The experience of combat deployment can be a difficult and painful one. It is common for people going through hardships to want to hurry up and get back to the way things were before. There are also times when people have feelings of doubt that things could ever be the same again.

After being in a war zone, many veterans may wonder if they will ever feel normal again. Veterans may have injuries and losses of physical capabilities; losses of comrades and friends; losses of time with children and separation from loved ones; losses of their job, occupation, or career; or losses of spouse through divorce. Other losses that veterans may experience in war include losses of innocence or losses of spiritual connectedness. The journey through the pain and grief resulting from such losses can be very difficult.

■ Section A: The meaning of hardships and challenges

When life is difficult, most of us ask one question—"why?" This question has been raised since the beginning of time. When we lose people who mean a lot to us, when we see others suffer, or when we experience our own loss, we need to know the reason for events that cause suffering and pain.

Indeed, most spiritual systems have tried to pinpoint the meaning of suffering and pain. There are many philosophies and religions that address this issue. An important point taken from all of these philosophies and religions is this:

■ Suffering and pain have the potential for creating greater possibilities and helping an individual to grow, should he or she choose to.

Identifying growth can be difficult for veterans who may be feeling depressed and worthless. Letting go of guilt and pain may feel like a betrayal to those who were lost. Veterans who are suffering from depression may have particular difficulty focusing on the positive. If you are still grieving and feel unable to complete this chapter, you should get additional help for depression and grief from a professional, and you may need to wait a little while before finishing this chapter. On the other hand, it is important to remember that it is human nature to avoid difficult topics. As you remember from Chapter 1, avoiding these topics will only maintain your stress symptoms. We encourage you to directly address these topics.

Identifying growth and strengths is often difficult to do for veterans who may be grieving or depressed. Additionally, veterans feel an alliance to their friends in war. Letting go of guilt and pain may feel like a betrayal to those who were lost. It may be helpful for the counselor or therapist to address these issues with the veteran.

Meaning making

Getting through hardships such as difficult war deployments is admirable, but what happens afterward? What do you do with those experiences now? Work hard at trying to forget everything? Live your life filled with bitterness and anger? Or do you become more understanding of life? Do you become wiser? How do you make meaning out of the experiences you have seen and lived through? Is it possible to transform and actually grow from surviving the hardships of your war experience?

If we look at others who have survived very difficult experiences, we find that most say that many good things have actually happened as a result of their dealing with hardships. This applies to war veterans as well as those who have suffered from other types of severe loss.

■ Section B: Identifying strengths

In addition to problems of combat stress, warriors also return with skills, knowledge, confidence, and a sense of accomplishment that only comes from surviving great hardship and overcoming challenges. Veterans have gained strength, worldliness, confidence, and sometimes even an appreciation for life that they never had before.

Take a look at and answer the following questions about your war experience:

■ What types of lessons or new skills did you learn while you were at war? What types of positive things did you accomplish?

■ What do you see as being your strengths?

■ How do you see yourself using those strengths in the near future?

Many veterans may benefit from assistance identifying skills and positive characteristics they have gained through their time of military service. For example, even though many combat-related skills may not be useful in other contexts, many other related characteristics may develop—for example, maturity, leadership skills, and the ability to quickly synthesize information and make difficult decisions.

Often, this process of beginning to recognize positive changes and positive skills and attributes gained during military experience is a part of the veterans overall broadening of their outlook. Specifically, often veterans return from combat remembering only the suffering, fear, or anger associated with a deployment. Often they experience difficulty in looking beyond some of the blatantly negative outcomes that they witnessed.

However, veterans often experience and recognize true growth when they begin to be able to see other aspects of their experience—for example, the value of the camaraderie, the development of fortitude and commitment, their own ability to persevere, the value of their own courage and beliefs, or their own commitment to creating positive changes and helping others.

■ Section C: Identifying values

Our values are the qualities in life that are most important to us. Even though we all have values that guide the way we live our lives, we rarely take a moment to think about what our values are. Values can refer to what is most important in our lives, such as an appreciation of:

- Your freedom,
- Your country,
- Your friends,
- Your family, and
- Your God.

As one example, many prisoners of war (POWs) from World War II faced long periods of severe stress, lost friends, and lost years with their families (who may have even assumed they were dead). However, despite the pain and the obvious losses experienced by these heroes, most survivors also said that they grew in some way from being a POW. Values that former POWs gained from their experiences of being in war included:

1. Greater appreciation for freedom,
2. Greater appreciation for family and friends,
3. Greater patience and understanding,
4. More optimism about life, and
5. The ability to know what is important in life, versus what is trivial.

Other amazing individuals note positive aspects to similar extraordinarily difficult circumstances. Senator John McCain, during his service in the U.S. Navy, received numerous honors—including a Bronze Star, Silver Star, the Legion of Merit,

Purple Heart, and the Distinguished Flying Cross. Despite enduring incredible hardship including frequent torture during five and a half years as a POW during the Vietnam War, he has spoken positively in interviews about his experiences saying, "I was privileged to observe a thousand acts of courage and compassion and love." He also demonstrates a strong commitment to these values: "To sacrifice for a cause greater than yourself, and to sacrifice your life to the eminence of that cause, is the noblest activity of all."

Everett Alvarez Jr. was the first naval aviator shot down over Vietnam during the Vietnam War, and was held as a POW for eight and half years, enduring hardship and torture until his release in 1973. Mr. Alvarez received numerous awards during his military career, including the Silver Star, two Bronze Stars, two Legions of Merit, two Purple Hearts, and the Distinguished Flying Cross. During an interview for the *Pittsburgh Post Gazette* in 2001 (Uricchio, 2001), he was asked how his time as a POW changed him. He responded:

> It was a maturing process. In order to survive the harshness, the terrible things we had to go through, we had to hold onto our core values and beliefs. In doing so, it was a tempering process of our characters. When you come out, you recognize there are obstacles in life, but you work your way through them and press on. You recognize also what's most important in life, and that's having your family and those you love around you. Material wealth is not as important, certainly not as important as health. You recognize how short life is, and how little time you have to go out and do something not only for yourself but for others.

He was also asked if he was angry about having lost over eight years of his life, and said:

> You know, one of the things you learn is that life is full of unexpected occurrences. I could be very angry, but what good would that do? I've always taken the attitude that you look forward and thank God you have your life because a lot of people don't. I have the opportunity to go on and continue my life. It would not behoove me to look back.

Mr. Alvarez has served as the deputy director of the Peace Corps and deputy administrator of the Veterans Administration, as well as founding his own management consulting firm and co-authoring two books. In his book, *Chained Eagle*—an account of his experiences in Vietnam—Alvarez (2005) writes, "My strength came from holding fast to my faith in God and belief in the values enshrined in our Constitution: duty, loyalty, unity, integrity, honor, allegiance, courage and hope" (p. 2).

Often situations that produce severe hardship can also produce positive changes and opportunities for growth. This growth can take many forms, including an increase in commitment to positive values.

Values also include principles we live our lives by, such as:

- Being honest
- Doing a good job
- Being a reliable son or daughter

- Being a model citizen
- Being a good parent or spouse or partner
- Respecting elders
- Being a loyal friend

Take some time to think about and answer the following questions:

- What are some important things you have learned from surviving your deployment?

  _____

  _____

  _____

- What kinds of things do you value more now that you have come back from the war?

  _____

  _____

  _____

- List three of the most important values in your life:

  _____

  _____

  _____

We rarely take the time to think about our values. However, the closer we follow our values in our day-to-day lives, the more meaningful our lives can be. For example, one Iraq War veteran said that seeing so much suffering while deployed—and being apart from his family—made him value being a good parent to his young daughter. When he returned home, he recognized that he had lost important friends while in Iraq, and he also recognized the importance of developing close relationships with other friends and loves ones. And because he valued being a good parent, he did his best to:

- Spend time with his daughter.
- Speak to his daughter in a respectful way.
- Attend school meetings.
- Help teach his daughter positive life lessons.

For each of the values you listed above, write down exactly how a person who has that value might behave. What would such a person do?

Value	How would a person who has this value behave?
Value No. 1	1.
	2.
	3.
	4.
Value No. 2	1.
	2.
	3.
	4.
Value No. 3	1.
	2.
	3.
	4.

Identifying values can also be difficult for a depressed veteran to do. The veteran will likely benefit from assistance identifying their values, related behaviors, as well as a discussion of just how they might apply these behaviors in their own lives.

■ Section D: Identifying goals

Your goals are the aims or objectives you have for yourself. However, rarely do we sit back and think about what goals we have for our lives and which goals might be best for us. Goals that are best for us will be consistent with our values and will help us meet our needs in some way. What do you want to achieve with your life?

Before you went to war, you may have had goals for what you wanted to accomplish in life. Goals might have included:

- Getting a good job
- Learning a trade
- Getting a college degree
- Getting married
- Having children

- What goals did you have for yourself *before* you went to war?

  _____
  _____
  _____

- Have these goals changed?

  _____
  _____
  _____

- List three goals that you have for your life now:

  _____
  _____
  _____

There are many goals in life that we dream about. For example, when you were young you might have had a goal to become a millionaire. As adults, it is important for us to choose goals that really make sense and that are achievable. Additionally, you must choose a goal that you are willing to work toward. When you have a short-term goal, you must be willing to complete the work that it takes to reach it. For example, imagine that a veteran named Bill wants to complete four college courses. He must show up for class, pay attention in class, complete homework, and study for exams.

When we have a long-term goal, we choose behaviors that help us reach those goals. For example, if Bill wants to get a college degree, he must first take the courses he needs to qualify for college. He must obtain the finances to pay for college. And he must complete all the courses that are required for his degree.

For at least one of the goals you listed above, write down exactly what steps need to be taken to reach that goal.

Goal	What steps should a person who has this goal take?
Goal No. 1	1.
	2.
	3.
	4.
Goal No. 2	1.
	2.
	3.
	4.
Goal No. 3	1.
	2.
	3.
	4.

If you are grieving or suffering from depression it may be difficult for you to set goals. Do your best. Again, those who are still grieving and feel unable to complete this chapter should see a professional who can provide help for their depression and grief, and may need to wait a little while before finishing this chapter.

Following highly stressful events, some individuals may feel hopeless or apathetic about setting goals. In this segment, it may be important to recognize these are expected reactions. The veteran will likely benefit from encouragement as they identify old and/or new positive goals, as well as exploration of what steps to take in their day-to-day life to meet their goals.

Also take time, as the program is concluded, to reinforce the positive work accomplished by the veteran. During the course of this program they have learned new skills, likely begun to reincorporate positive healthy behaviors that may have been lost for a time, and also focused on training new habits that may help them readjust from their wartime experience. However, it is also essential for veterans to know that ongoing improvement requires *ongoing* focus and training. Just as they improved during the course of this program, they can continue to improve by using the same techniques they have been practicing, and continuing to apply the same principles that they learned.

▶ When to talk to your doctor

Have you or someone you know been:

- Feeling trapped, suffocated, closed-in, or panicky when you are in closed-in areas or crowds?
- Feeling angry at or disconnected from others, or like no one can understand what you are going through?
- Feeling overwhelmed by your reactions?
- Thinking you might hurt yourself or someone else?

Did the veteran answer YES to ONE or more of these questions? If so, have them talk to their doctor right away.

▶ The heart of the matter

Your war deployment(s) will likely be among the most significant experiences of your life. Many veterans from other eras often feel that their combat experience played a critical role in their developing into a mature adult with positive character and strong values. Often they describe their war experiences as including some of the *best* experiences of their lives—even if going to war also included the *worst* experiences of their lives.

Your view of the world is now different. Your view of yourself and others will now be different. It will take time to see the broader significance your role made to your country. Over time you will gain the perspective to understand how immensely profound this experience really has been, and how much strength you truly possess.

Remember to ask the veteran to complete the quiz at the end of the chapter:

- Please turn to the end of the chapter and take the quiz.

▶ On your own

It is now time to put together all the skills you learned from this book. Continue to use the skills you learned in your everyday life. Remember to set positive goals for different ways that you can challenge yourself each day—daily practice, daily training, and daily healing.

▶ Further readings for the clinician

Alvarez, E., & Pitch, A. S. (2005). *Chained eagle: The heroic story of the first American shot down over North Vietnam.* Washington, DC: Potomac Books.

Alvarez, E., & Schreiner, S. A. (1991). *Code of conduct.* New York: D. I. Fine

Dahl, J., & Lundgren, T. (2006). *Living beyond your pain: Using acceptance and commitment therapy to ease chronic pain.* Oakland, CA: New Harbinger.

Calhoun, L., & Tedeschi, R. G. (Eds.). (1999). *Facilitating posttraumatic growth: A clinician's guide.* Mahwah, NJ: Lawrence Erlbaum.

Hayes, S. C. (2005). *Get out of your mind and into your life: The new acceptance and commitment therapy.* Oakland, CA: New Harbinger.

Walser, R. D., & Westrup, D. (2007). *Acceptance and commitment therapy for the treatment of post-traumatic stress disorder and trauma related problems: A practitioner's guide to using mindfulness and acceptance strategies.* Oakland, CA: New Harbinger.

Name: _____

Date: _____ _____ / _____ _____ / _____ _____

1. List four positive things that you learned about yourself when you were deployed (e.g., courage, ability to protect yourself, discipline).

    1. _____
    2. _____
    3. _____
    4. _____

2. What do you want your life to look like five years from now? Name four goals you have for yourself.

    1. _____
    2. _____
    3. _____
    4. _____

3. In this chapter, you identified some of your values, and ways a person who has those values might behave. Name some things you can do in the weeks and months ahead, that are consistent with your values?

    1. _____
    2. _____
    3. _____
    4. _____

Clinician Resource Guide

► Veteran Affairs (VA) resources

■ VA medical centers

The VA Medical Center system's specialized PTSD clinics and programs can provide to eligible veterans educational information, diagnostic assessment and treatment for PTSD and other mental health and medical disorders. Following deployment to a combat zone after discharge, if a returnee has enrolled for VA services, he or she should be qualified for two years of care for conditions potentially related to your service. Both VA medical centers and Vet Centers provide veterans with mental-health services that health insurance will cover or that costs little or nothing, according to a veteran's ability to pay. To find a VA Medical Center near you, call 1-800-905-4675 or look on the web at www1.va.gov/directory/guide/home.asp?isFlash=1.

■ Vet centers

Community-based Vet Centers provide benefits information, evaluations, and treatment for trauma to any veteran who served in a war zone or in a military conflict (such as in Panama, Grenada, or Somalia). There are no co-payments or charges of any kind for Vet Center confidential services. Vet Centers also provide trauma counseling for veterans who were sexually harassed or sexually assaulted while on active duty. To find a Vet Center near you, call 1-800-905-4675 or look on the web also at www1.va.gov/directory/guide/home.asp?isFlash=1.

■ Tragedy Assistance Program for Survivors (TAPS)

The Tragedy Assistance Program for Survivors (TAPS) is a nonprofit Veterans Service Organization that provides a wide range of free services to all those affected by the death of a loved one in the armed forces. To find a TAPS program call 1-800-959-TAPS (1-800-959-8277) or look on the web at www.TAPS.org.

■ Office of Veterans services

The Office of Veterans Services Acts as a liaison between the Department of Veterans Affairs and individual veterans and between the governor and veterans' organizations. Assist veterans in obtaining State and federal entitlements, supply the latest information on veterans' issues and provide advice and support to veterans making the transition back into civilian life.

■ VA benefits

To find out more about VA health benefits, call 1-877-222-VETS. The web provides information about VA Medical Center in your area at www.va.gov/rcs/. The VA also offers the MyHealtheVet and Seamless Transition web sites, full of helpful online information for veterans and family members.

▶ Military resources

Clients who are Active Duty can access their installation's support services for information about where to find mental health services. Larger installations will have a military treatment facility on-site that may provide treatment for PTSD. Many of these centers provide individual, group, marriage, and family counseling. These might include:

- Air Force Life Skills Clinics
- Army Community Centers
- Marine Corps Community Services
- U.S. Coast Guard Work-Life Center

Additionally, family programs may be available to support to families in military and civilian settings. Such centers also can provide information and updates on available benefits, entitlements, and services (medical care, etc.). These might include:

- Airman and Family Readiness Programs
- Army Family Advocacy Programs
- Army National Guard
- State Family Program Office
- Fleet and Family Support Center
- Marine & Family Services Counseling Services

■ Military ONESOURCE

An organization that provides services including brief counseling to active duty military personnel, including Reservists and the National Guard (1-800-342-9647; www.military-onesource.com).

▶ Community resources

Important questions to ask a potential therapist include:

- What experience do you have working with war returnees with trauma and or PTSD?
- Do you have any specialized training in PTSD treatment?
- What kinds of PTSD treatments do you use?

Here are some websites that can help to locate a qualified therapist in your area:

- **The Association for Advancement of Behavioral and Cognitive Therapies** (ABCT, formerly AABT) is a professional organization that maintains a referral source for therapists with advanced training in Cognitive Behavioral Therapy. You can also list the area you need special help with, such as PTSD, to locate a therapist with special expertise. They are located on the web at www.abct.org.
- **Sidran** is a nonprofit trauma organization that offers a referral list of professional therapists, as well as a fact sheet on how to choose a therapist for PTSD and dissociative disorders at www.sidran.org.
- **The American Psychological Association** also offers a list of referrals by area at http://locator.apa.org/terms.cfm.
- *Psychology Today* lists therapists at http://therapists.psychologytoday.com/ppc/prof_search.php?iorb=4764/.
- **Community Mental Health Centers** may be available in your area. You can find a center near you at the Center for Mental Health Services Locator site at www.mentalhealth.samhsa.gov/databases/.

Finally, another way to locate a therapist is to make phone calls in your area to:

- Your local mental-health agency or family physician.
- Your local state psychological association.
- A local university or college department of psychology.
- If you are a member of a Health Maintenance Organization (HMO), call to find out if mental-health services are available.

▶ Web resources

The National Center for Post-Traumatic Stress Disorder is a comprehensive source for information related to PTSD developed by leaders in the field of PTSD. The website contains over 200 pages, 125 fact sheets, 400 downloadable articles, videos, and a searchable database of 25,000+ articles at National Center for Post-Traumatic Stress Disorder: www.ncptsd.va.org.

The Iraqi War Clinician's Guide in a treatment guide developed collaboratively by top clinicians and researchers in the Department of Defense and the National Center for PTSD. The guide contains numerous articles on the assessment and treatment of OIF/OEF returnees. It is an excellent resource for clinicians who are addressing various issues posed by returnees. You can find it on the NC-PTSD website at www.ncptsd.va.org.

Battlemind.org training helps recent returning veterans to develop a realistic preview, in the form of a briefing, of the stresses and strains of deployment on Soldiers. It is developed by leading military professionals at Walter Reed Army Institute of Research. Four training briefs are available for soldiers, leaders, National Guard/Reserves, and families at www.battlemind.org.

Courage to Care is an electronic health campaign for military and civilian professionals serving the military community, as well as for military men, women and families. Courage to Care at www.usuhs.mil/psy/courage.html consists of electronic fact sheets on health topics relevant to military life. Courage to Care content is developed by leading military health experts from Uniformed Services University of the Health Sciences, your nation's federal medical school.

Another good online resource is *webmd.com*. Veterans can go into this site and search for stress management techniques. It has hundreds of additional resources at www.webmd.com.

Chapter Outlines

▶ Chapter 1—Outline

■ Understanding Transition Stress Reactions

Session Topics and Goals

Background

Section A: Types of combat stress reactions

Section B: Stress and the brain

Section C: The problem of avoidance

Section D: Monitoring stress

Section E: Grounding and relaxation techniques

Section F: Treatments for transition stress reactions

Background

- Describe goals of the program, and of the first session.
- Begin to normalize a broad range of war-related stress reactions.
- Highlight the process of healing and recovering from highly stressful events and situations.

Section A: Types of combat stress reactions

- Ask veteran(s) to name/describe specific combat-stress reactions they have experienced.
- Discuss types of common combat stress reactions.
- Normalize common reactions to highly stressful events.
- Help veterans understand their combat stress reactions in the context of categories of reactions:

    —Reexperiencing—ways that the mind and body "replay" the event.

    —Hypervigilance—including strong emotional and physical reactions, such as feeling "amped" and hypervigiliant.

    —Avoidance/Numbing—ways of trying to decrease symptoms by avoiding reminders, as well as becoming emotionally numb.

- Reemphasize that veterans are experiencing normal reactions to abnormal stressors.

Section B: Stress and the brain

- Emphasize that veterans reactions are the result of body/brain reactions to extreme stress, and that these reactions are learned by the system (the body and brain).
- Explain how the brain-body "system" helps us deal with situational threats or stressors.
- Describe the role of the amygdala in coping with stress.
- Discuss how reactions relate to signal-noise ratio in accurately analyzing stressful situations.

Section C: The problem of avoidance

- Further discuss the role of avoidance in coping with war-related stress.
- Explain how the use of avoidance hinders the healing process, and how it trains the amygdala to fear things which may not be dangerous.
- Emphasize the importance of engaging in new experiences, to essentially re-train the brain (specifically, the amygdala) to recognize real versus inaccurately perceived threats.

Section D: Monitoring stress

- Discuss the importance of veterans monitoring their internal stress levels.
- Describe for veterans the SUDS and how to apply it to keeping their stress levels in check.
- Help veterans practice using the SUDS to monitor stress reactions in session.

Section E: Grounding and relaxation techniques

- Describe for the veterans one technique to help lower stress, belly or diaphragmatic breathing.
- Practice technique with them in session, and obtain pre- and post-SUDS levels with use of this particular technique.

Section F: Treatments for transition stress reactions

- Inform veterans of best-practice treatments for dealing with after-war stress, including CBT and medication.
- Advise the veterans to seek out care by a professional as needed.

When to talk to your doctor

Assignment:

1. Encourage veterans to review the specific combat stress reaction types, and identify issues that have been particularly uncomfortable or disruptive in their lives. It

will also be helpful for veterans to begin noticing specific cues for their reactions, to better predict when each coping strategies will be most useful.

2. Complete the Phone Calling Exercise, using the Calling Exercise Sheet. Have veterans write down their SUDS before each call and after each call, as well as the duration of each call.

3. Begin to practice using the Grounding and Relaxation techniques during the coming week.

▶ Chapter 2—Outline

■ Managing Stress

Session Topics and Goals

Review of homework

Background

Section A: Unmanaged stress

Section B: Coping with and managing stress

Section C: Treatments for stress and anxiety

Review of homework

- Review homework for phone calling exercise from Chapter 1.

- Review homework for grounding exercises.

- Check in with veterans regarding areas they focused on and skills they practiced.

- If some individuals did not practice the assignment, address factors that interfered with practice and emphasize the importance of daily practice.

Section A: Unmanaged stress

- Reemphasize that veterans' reactions to after-war stress are normal, considering what they have gone through.

- Provide veterans with common physical symptoms of stress.

- Provide veterans with common symptoms of emotional and mental stress.

- Help veterans to identify triggers for their stress reactions, utilizing the Identifying Stress Cues Worksheet.

- Talk with veterans about how prolonged stress affects the brain and body.

Section B: Coping with and managing stress

- Normalize veterans' reactions to stress after returning from war.

- Explore how veterans can manage their stress.

- Provide veterans with techniques to help manage their physical and emotional stress.

- Differentiate and provide veteran with body-centered and mind-centered techniques to manage stress.
- Describe progressive muscle relaxation.
- Practice technique with them in session, and obtain pre- and post-SUDS levels with use of this particular technique.

Section C: Treatments for stress and anxiety

- Provide various treatments utilized for managing stress, including: biofeedback, body awareness training, relaxation exercises, and other coping skills we discussed in this chapter.

When to talk to your doctor

Assignment:

1. Have veterans use the **Weekly Stress Monitoring Worksheet** to monitor progress in managing their stress.
2. Have veterans pick a stress management technique, and to put it on the **Stress Management Schedule.**
3. Have veterans continue to practice the Phone Calling Exercise.

▶ Chapter 3—Outline

■ Tools for Healthy Coping

Session Topics and Goals

Review of homework

Background

Section A: Reactive and proactive coping strategies

Section B: Depression and the danger of doing nothing

Section C: Negative coping, negative mood

Section D: Positive action, positive mood

Section E: Common pitfalls

Section F: Putting coping activities in action

Section G: Treatments for transition stress

Review of homework

- Briefly review the assignment from Chapter 2.
- Check in with veterans regarding their use of the activity schedule.
- If some individuals did not practice the assignment, address factors that interfered with practice and emphasize the importance of daily practice.

Section A: Reactive and proactive coping strategies

■ Discuss the difference between reactive and proactive coping strategies.

■ Emphasize importance of the veteran committing to using proactive coping behaviors in his/her life.

Section B: Depression and the danger of doing nothing

■ Discuss with veterans how having negative thoughts relate to being more depressed.

■ Provide veterans with an overview of Beck and Lewinsohn's theories of depression.

■ Describe how depression can affect the veterans, and discuss how this can lead to a downward spiral of depression.

Section C: Negative coping, negative mood

■ Provide veterans with examples of negative coping responses.

■ Describe for veterans how this may play out in their day-to-day life.

Section D: Positive action, positive mood

■ Explain how positive coping behaviors help break the downward spiral of depression for the veterans.

■ Provide veterans with a variety of positive coping responses to dealing with stress.

■ Break down positive coping responses into four categories, to include: (1) body-focused activities, such as physical exercises, and mind-body exercises like meditation or deep breathing exercises; (2) goal-focused activities, such as doing projects or learning new skill; (3) social activities, such as going out and doing something with a friend; and (4) other positive activities, such as journaling, doing something creative, hobbies, or just doing something relaxing.

■ Have veterans write down a positive coping activity to do from each of the four categories during the week.

Section E: Common pitfalls

■ Discuss common reasons why veterans would not engage in positive coping behaviors.

■ Review each of those reasons, which include: feeling numb, avoidance, having no motivation, injuries, and experiencing significant life changes.

Section F: Putting coping activities into action

■ Help veterans break down activities and accomplish their goals.

Section G: Treatments for transition stress

- Inform the veterans of treatments for dealing with transition stress and decreasing depression.

When to talk to your doctor

Assignment:

1. Have veterans decide which positive coping activities they will do, and help them break those activities down into manageable goals.
2. Have veterans identify one activity per category to practice in the week ahead.
3. Have veterans complete the coping activity schedule to plan out their week.

▶ **Chapter 4—Outline**

■ **Improving Sleep**

Session Topics and Goals

Overview of sleep problems for veterans

Review of homework

Background—What are sleep problems?

Section A: Stages of sleep

Section B: How poor sleep habits can lead to sleep problems

Section C: Good sleep habits

Section D: Nightmares and night terrors

Section E: Treatments for sleep problems

Review of homework

- Briefly review the assignment from Chapter 3.
- Check in with veterans regarding their use of the activity schedule.
- If some individuals did not practice the assignment, address factors that interfered with practice and emphasize the importance of daily practice.

Background—What are sleep problems?

- Introduce the topic, "Improving Sleep"
- Discuss and normalize sleep problems experienced by the veterans.

Section A: Stages of sleep

- Review the Sleep Stages handout (Appendix C).
- Describe brain and body functioning during wakefulness and sleep stages.

Optional section—Sleep regulation

- Describe circadian rhythms and the sleep homeostat.
- Describe how these systems can be utilized to help promote sleep.

Section B: How poor sleep habits can lead to sleep problems

- Review common combat stress reactions that contribute to sleep problems:

    —Feeling hypervigilant or "on guard."

    —Distressing thoughts and images; nightmares.

- Avoiding going to bed because of increased symptoms. Also describe common ineffective strategies. For example:

    —Napping or going to bed early to "catch up on sleep."

    —Using alcohol to induce sleep.

    —Trying too hard—anxiety and fear of insomnia can exacerbate insomnia.

Section C: Good sleep habits

- Discuss patterns of sleep-promoting habits that can be practiced throughout the day.
- Ask veterans to choose a habit from each part of the day to practice in the coming week.
- Nighttime:

    —Developing specific "sleep rituals."

    —Creating a comfortable and peaceful bedroom environment.

    —Reserving bedroom only for sleep and sexual activity.

- Morning:

    —Set a regular time to wake up and begin the day, preferably with an enjoyable activity.

    —Increase sun/light exposure early in the day.

- Daytime:

    —Use brief naps (10–30 minutes) to improve mood, alertness, and mental performance.

    —Limit caffeine, nicotine, and alcohol use.

    —Exercise regularly; begin practicing overall stress management.

Section D: Nightmares and night terrors

- Normalize the experience of nightmares and night terrors following combat experience.
- Address harmful approaches to managing nightmares and suggest alternative approaches:

    —Once awake and re-oriented, practice a sleep ritual.

    —Seek support from a safe and supportive person.

Section E: Treatments for sleep problems

- Describe available treatments.

- Provide information regarding indicators that additional treatment may be needed.

When to talk to your doctor

Assignment:

Encourage veterans to identify three new sleep habits they are willing to try for the next three weeks, and to begin practicing new sleep habits using the **Sleep Habits Schedule** provided in their workbook.

▶ Chapter 5—Outline

■ Dealing with Anger

Session Topics and Goals

Review of homework

Background—Combat and anger

Section A: What is anger?

Section B: Risks and benefits from anger

Section C: How can I prevent harmful anger?

Section D: Treatments for anger

Review of homework

- Review Phone Calling Exercise.

- Review good sleep habits, and the veterans' completion of the Sleep Habits Schedule.

- If some individuals did not practice the assignment, address factors that interfered with practice and emphasize the importance of daily practice.

Background—Combat and anger

- Introduce the topic of dealing with anger, including the reality of anger being adaptive in a combat environment.

- Discuss and normalize typical struggles associated with managing anger following return from combat experience.

Section A: What is anger?

- Normalize anger feels as a part of normative combat stress reactions.

- Discuss types of anger.

- Explore physical and cognitive signs of anger escalation.

- Outline physiology of anger.
- Ask veterans to note their own anger signs (workbook).
- Highlight that anger is neither good nor bad, although our reactions may be.

Section B: Risks and benefits from anger

- Discuss risks associated with anger, including:
  —Physical.
  —Cognitive.
  —Interpersonal.
- Review potential benefits of anger, which may help:
  —People reach goals.
  —Motivate people to work harder.
  —People solve problems.
  —People handle emergencies with a burst of energy.
  —People successfully accomplish dangerous missions.
- Have veterans list health ways they can channel their anger (workbook).

Section C: How can I prevent harmful anger?

- Teach the Anger Scale for monitoring anger level.
  —Ask veterans to rate their own anger level (workbook).
- Discuss rationale and method for time-out.
  —Use time-out sheet in workbook.
  —Ask veterans to answer questions regarding use of time-out (workbook).
- Discuss healthy ways to resolve anger.
  —Veterans should list approaches they can practice (workbook).

Section D: Treatments for anger

- Describe available treatments.
- Provide information regarding indicators that additional treatment may be needed.

When to talk to your doctor

Assignment:

1. Complete the Phone Calling Exercise.
2. Identify a possible future situation where you may have to deal with your anger:
   - What are the clues to look for—physically, emotionally, or otherwise—that will let you know that you are becoming angry?
   - What are some healthy things that you can do to help resolve the situation?
   - Practice using the time-out technique. Plan ahead, by thinking about the type of situations you might need a time-out, and how you will implement it.

■ Reintegrating with Society

Session Topics and Goals

Review of homework

Background—Reintegration

Section A: Major reintegration issue—Control

Section B: Major reintegration issue—Hypervigilance

Section C: Major reintegration issue—Coping with civilians

Section D: Treatments for reintegration difficulties

Review of homework

- Briefly review Phone Calling Exercise.
- Review with the veterans their plans to manage anger in specific situations they identified as high risk, their overall use of anger management skills, and specific use of the time-out technique.
- If some individuals did not practice the assignment, address factors that interfered with practice and emphasize the importance of daily practice.

Background—Reintegration

- Introduce the topic of reintegration, acknowledging the struggles that characterize re-transition stress.
- Elicit from the veterans a number of individual specific problems they have been experiencing, recognizing commonness among experiences, and encouraging positive coping.

Section A: Major reintegration issue—Control

- Normalize feelings of not being in control of some factors in life.
- Discuss factors within individual's control, and things beyond their control.

Section B: Major reintegration issue—Hypervigilance

- Define vigilance and hypervigilance.
- Normalize feelings of hypervigilance following combat, recognizing its adaptive nature while in combat, and long-term risks while in a safer environment.
- Discuss graduated practice of re-acclimating to other environments that may initially trigger hypervigilance (e.g., social situations or going out in public).

Section C: Major reintegration issue—Coping with civilians

- Discuss culture-shock associated with retransition (including due to changes occurring at home while service members were deployed, feeling that everyday life is now trivial, etc.).

- Discuss the reality of insensitive/provocative/offensive questions or statements from others (e.g., friends, family members, and strangers).

- Monitor levels of anger in veteran(s)—this may be a good time to review time-outs.

- Complete the Reintegration Plan Worksheet, encouraging a move towards positive coping.

- Elicit from veterans specific communication problems they have experienced, and help devise more effective communication approaches for these situations.

- Encourage ongoing use of the Reintegration Plan Worksheet.

Section D: Treatments for reintegration difficulties

- Describe available treatments.

- Provide information regarding indicators that additional treatment may be needed.

When to talk to your doctor

Assignment:

1. Complete the Phone Calling Exercise.

2. Use the Reintegration Plan Worksheet in this chapter to plan what you will do to cope with people who trigger anger or stress. Continue to practice good communication and time-out skills with others. Keep using your new skills, and you will find that things go more smoothly when there are problems.

▶ Chapter 7—Outline

■ Reintegrating with Family and Friends

Session Topics and Goals

Review of homework

Background—The important role of families and friends

Section A: Connecting with your family and friends

Section B: Special issues for couples and children

Section C: Suggestions for reintegration

Section D: Dealing with the change

Section E: "Fighting fair"

Section F: Communication plan worksheet

Section G: Treatments for relationship difficulties

Review of homework

- Briefly review the Phone Calling Exercise.
- Review with veterans the Reintegration Plan Worksheet they filled out to plan how to cope with people/situations that trigger anger or stress.
- Check in with veterans regarding their ongoing practice of good communications and time-out skills with others.
- If some individuals did not practice the assignment, address factors that interfered with practice and emphasize the importance of daily practice.

Background—The important role of families and friends

- Provide background regarding the role of family members in providing companionship, sense of belonging, esteem, support, etc.
- Acknowledge the stress associated with experiencing difficulties reconnecting with valued family members and friends.

Section A: Connecting with your family and friends

- Discuss common reactions among veterans (e.g., loss of interest in activities, difficulty trusting or feeling close to others, need for control, difficulties showing. emotions other than anger, or not wanting to share experiences with family members).
- Discuss and normalize relationship problems associated with these common reactions.
- Discuss and normalize typical problems currently being experienced by veterans.

Section B: Special issues for couples and children

- Discuss typical problems experienced by couples during the transition period (e.g., difficulties with face to face communication, sexual intimacy, veterans feeling closer to buddies than spouse, or changes in roles/responsibilities/outlook/priorities).
- Discuss common retransition problems related to children (e.g., children having changed/grown up during the veteran's absence, children being slow to warm up to a returning parent or showing other apparent ambivalence or neediness).
- Discuss veterans' expectations regarding their return, and normalize various reactions (e.g., expectations that the transition would be very smooth, feelings of disappointment, worry that things will not get better).

Section C: Suggestions for reintegration

■ Present suggestions listed in chapter for reintegration with family and friends (e.g., making individual time to listen to each valued person, taking time to renew relationship with spouse or partner, going slowly in reestablishing one's place in the family, taking time to spend with buddies, sharing some stories with family, remaining flexible in re-negotiating family roles and routines).

Section D: Dealing with the change

■ Help veterans focus on their own role in handling difficult changes, with 3 steps:

1. Normalizing current reactions.
2. Recalling from Chapter 2 the types of social interactions that help people feel good, and making a list of people likely to provide positive interactions.
3. Actually talking to these people, and accepting support from them.

Section E: "Fighting fair"

■ Discuss the importance to a relationship of being able to disagree, and resolve disagreements.
■ Rules for "fighting fair":
—Plan ahead.
—Keep your eyes on the prize.
—Use "I."
—Stick to one topic.
—Stay calm.
—No "below the belt" shots.

Section F: Communication Plan Worksheet

■ Complete and discuss the Communication Plan Worksheet.

Section G: Treatments for relationship difficulties

■ Describe available treatments.
■ Provide information regarding indicators that additional treatment may be needed.

When to talk to your doctor

Assignment:

1. Complete the Phone Calling Exercise.
2. Your Communication Plan Worksheet is your master plan for dealing with conflicts. If you are ready, go ahead and bring up any problem(s) you identified with

your family members or friends. You can copy this worksheet or answer these questions in your head when you run into problems with anyone. Use this sheet to have a conversation with someone this week.

▶ Chapter 8—Outline

■ Staying Strong

Session Topics and Goals

Review of homework

Background—Building strength

Section A: The meaning of hardships and challenges

Section B: Identifying strengths

Section C: Identifying values

Section D: Identifying goals

Review of homework

- Review the Phone Calling Exercise.

- Briefly review with group members the Communication Plan Worksheet they filled out to plan for dealing with conflicts.

- Check in with veterans regarding their practice of addressing specific problems with family members or friends, and their ongoing use of communications and time-out skills.

- If some individuals did not practice the assignment, address factors that interfered with practice and emphasize the importance of daily practice.

Background—Building strength

- Briefly discuss the reality of the hardships associated with surviving and recovering from combat deployment, as well as the tremendous human ability to grow from our challenges.

Section A: The meaning of hardships and challenges

- Discuss the common human question ("Why?"), asked in response to pain and suffering, and the issue of making meaning from experiences.

- Discuss the potential for growth that comes from struggling with pain and change, and discerning the significance of having survived war.

Section B: Identifying strengths

- Discuss with the group skills and accomplishments they gained from their military and wartime experience.

- What do veterans see as their strengths, and how can they use them productively in the future?

Section C: Identifying values

- Discuss values we may hold in general (e.g., being honest, reliable, and loyal; being a good parent and spouse; doing a good job; respecting elders; appreciating God, freedom, our country, family, and friends).

- What have veterans learned from surviving their deployment—what kinds of things do they value more now, and what is most important in their life now?

Section D: Identifying goals

- Discuss goals held before the war (e.g., getting a good job, learning a trade, college, having a family).

- How have goals changed? What are your goals now?

When to talk to your doctor

Assignment:

It is now time to put together all the skills you learned from this workbook. Continue to use the skills you learned in your everyday life.

Also, please complete the short review quiz on the next page.

Pre/Post Tests

Measuring veterans' progress will help them to see how much they improve over the course of this program. We include in this Appendix three surveys that evaluate three relevant areas: coping skills, content knowledge, and symptoms. We recommend administering these surveys as part of an assessment protocol to veterans before and after the intervention. We also welcome your sending pre- and post-intervention data to us along with the Clinican Follow-Up Questionnaire (Appendix F).

▶ CSI

Please read every question carefully. For each question, circle the answer that is closest to your experience.

1. How many times **in the past week** did you do something pleasant or enjoyable?
   a. Never (0)
   b. Once (1)
   c. 2 to 4 times a week (2)
   d. 4 to 6 times a week (3)
   e. 7 or more times a week (4)

2. How many times **in the past week** did you do something productive?
   a. Never (0)
   b. Once (1)
   c. 2 to 4 times a week (2)
   d. 4 to 6 times a week (3)
   e. 7 or more times a week (4)

3. How many times **in the past week** did you hang out with family or friends?
   a. Never (0)
   b. Once (1)
   c. 2 to 4 times a week (2)

    d. 4 to 6 times a week (3)

    e. 7 or more times a week (4)

4. How many times **in the past week** did you lose your temper?

    a. Never (4)

    b. Once (3)

    c. 2 to 4 times a week (2)

    d. 4 to 6 times a week (1)

    e. 7 or more times a week (0)

5. On average, on a scale of 1 to 10 (with 1 being very low levels of anger to 10 being explosive anger) what has your anger level been during **this past week?**

    a. 0 to 1 (4)

    b. 2 to 3 (3)

    c. 4 to 5 (2)

    d. 6 to 7 (1)

    e. 8 to 10 (0)

6. What percentage of time did you feel angry during **this past week?**

    a. 0 to 20 percent (4)

    b. 20 to 40 percent (3)

    c. 40 to 60 percent (2)

    d. 60 to 80 percent (1)

    e. 80 to 100 percent (0)

7. How many days did you wake up feeling rested during **this past week?**

    a. None (0)

    b. One day (1)

    c. 2 to 4 days (2)

    d. 4 to 6 days (3)

    e. 7 or more days (4)

8. On average, how many hours of sleep did you get *per night* during **this past week?**

    a. 0 to 1 hours (0)

    b. 1 to 3 hours (1)

    c. 3 to 5 hours (2)

    d. 5 to 7 hours (3)

    e. 7 or more hours (4)

9. How many times did you use any alcohol or drugs to help you fall asleep during **this past week?**

    a. Never (4)

    b. Once (3)

c. 2 to 4 times a week (2)

d. 4 to 6 times a week (1)

e. 7 or more times a week (0)

10. What percentage of time did you feel nervous, irritated, and/or on-edge during **this past week**?

  a. 0 to 20 percent (4)

  b. 20 to 40 percent (3)

  c. 40 to 60 percent (2)

  d. 60 to 80 percent (1)

  e. 80 to 100 percent (0)

11. What percentage of time did you feel calm and/or relaxed during **this past week**?

  a. 0 to 20 percent (0)

  b. 20 to 40 percent (1)

  c. 40 to 60 percent (2)

  d. 60 to 80 percent (3)

  e. 80 to 100 percent (4)

12. How many times did you do something healthy to help you feel more relaxed (for example yoga, watch a movie, read a novel/good book, take a fun vacation, get a massage, physical exercise) during **this past week**?

  a. Never (0)

  b. Once (1)

  c. 2 to 4 times a week (2)

  d. 4 to 6 times a week (3)

  e. 7 or more times a week (4)

■ CSI scoring instructions

Step 1: Look at your answers on the CSI. Each answer you circled had a number to the right of it. This number is the weight. Go to your CSI Scoring Worksheet (next page) and enter in the weights for each question number in the boxes provided for you.

Step 2: Add the weights for the four sets of questions (1–3 and 4–6 and 7–9 and 10–12). Write down each sum in the boxes under each set of questions.

Step 3: Finally, add up all of the sums together that you got in Step 2. Adding the four totals together will give you a grand total score for the CSI.

■ CSI scoring worksheet

	Question Number	Weight	Question Number	Weight	Question Number	Weight	Question Number	Weight
Step 1	1 2 3	▭ ▭ ▭	4 5 6	▭ ▭ ▭	7 8 9	▭ ▭ ▭	10 11 12	▭ ▭ ▭
Step 2	Positive Coping Skills	SUM (1-3) ⬇ ▭	Anger Management	SUM (4-6) ⬇ ▭	Sleep Hygiene	SUM (7-9) ⬇ ▭	Stress Management	SUM (10-12) ⬇ ▭
Step 3			Your Total Score for the *CSI*:	➡	▭			

■ What your CSI score means

If your score was between:

40 and 48: You are coping very well. You likely do not engage in unhealthy habits, such as isolating, drinking and/or using drugs to try to deal with your problems. You tend to communicate well with those around you, and deal with your anger in constructive ways. You are presently handling your stress well.

30 and 39: You are coping fairly well right now and make good efforts to take care of yourself. However, you may have some difficulties communicating with your family, friends, and other people in your life. You may have some problems at times controlling your anger and stress. You will benefit from learning more about how to cope with combat stress.

20 and 29: You are having some problems coping right now. You are struggling in many areas of your life, and are having a hard time taking good care of yourself. You may also be having trouble controlling your stress and anger. You use unhealthy coping methods and so we recommend that you learn more about how to cope with combat stress.

0 and 19: You are having a lot of problems coping right now. You may be struggling with emotional pain and need help coping. You are likely having a hard time managing your anger and may be having problems in your relationships with family, friends, and/or co-workers. You are likely using unhealthy coping several times per week, and your stress level is high. *It is important that you speak with your doctor* to get the help you need to cope right now.

▶ CKS

Please read every question carefully. Answer each question to the best of your ability.

1. What are some **common** reactions to the homecoming experience after being in the war zone?
   a. Getting irritated
   b. Feeling numb inside at first
   c. Thinking no one else understands
   d. All of these are expected reactions

2. Which of the following statements is an example of fighting fair?
   a. "I feel like you are always nagging me."
   b. "You always nag me when I watch TV."
   c. "I feel angry when you tell me not to watch TV because I need time to relax."
   d. All of the above are examples.

3. Which of the following is **true** about time-outs?
   a. They're only good for punishing children by placing them in a corner.
   b. Adults can't benefit from using them with each other.
   c. They're good for times when adults are being irrational.
   d. Time-outs are just a way to run away from the problem.

4. When we experience very few activities we consider to be pleasant or productive, we are more likely feel depressed. Also, when we feel depressed, we don't feel like doing the kinds of activities that are likely to make us feel better. **This is known as the:**
   a. Positive vicious cycle
   b. Downward spiral of depression
   c. Sliding depressive cycle
   d. Resilient coping

5. What are some **common** symptoms of long-term stress?

a. Irritability

b. Upset stomach, nausea, diarrhea

c. Stiff neck or headaches

d. All of these are common

6. What does **SUDS** stand for?

a. Strong Underpinnings of Denial and Suppression

b. Subjective Units of Distress Scale

c. Subjective Units of Damaging Stress

d. SoapscumSoap scum Under Da Sink in Hawaii

7. This is a relaxation technique where you breathe in with your belly coming out, and exhaling and your belly coming back in. It is very easy and helps people to relax. **What is it called?**

a. Auto-reflex breathing

b. Deep muscle breathing

c. Diaphragmatic breathing

d. Exhalation therapy

8. Being angry for long period of time may lead to:

a. High blood pressure

b. Early death

c. Stomach disorders

d. All of the above

9. It's very unusual to experience unwanted memories after returning from the war zone.

True or False

10. Anger is a "bad" emotion that can only lead to conflict and aggression.

True or False

11. We all have dreams every night that we sleep.

True or False

12. Antidepressants can mess up our sleep cycle.

True or False

13. Taking a 60-minute nap can mess up the sleep cycle.

True or False

14. If you can not fall asleep at night, it is best to do something highly stressful to make you tired and help you fall asleep.

True or False

15. Working all the time to try to avoid distressing war memories is a good way to deal with post-war stress.

True or False

1. What are some **common** reactions to the homecoming experience after being in the war zone?

   d. All of these are expected reactions

2. Which of the following statements is an example of fighting fair?

   c. "I feel angry when you tell me not to watch TV because I need time to relax."

3. Which of the following is **true** about time-outs?

   c. They're good for times when adults are being irrational.

4. When we experience very few activities we consider to be pleasant or productive, we are more likely feel depressed. Also, when we feel depressed, we don't feel like doing the kinds of activities that are likely to make us feel better. **This is known as the:**

   b. Downward spiral of depression

5. What are some **common** symptoms of long-term stress?

   d. All of these are common

6. What does **SUDS** stand for?

   b. Subjective Units of Distress Scale

7. This is a relaxation technique where you breathe in with your belly coming out, and exhaling and your belly coming back in. It is very easy and helps people to relax. **What is it called**?

   c. Diaphragmatic breathing

8. Being angry for long period of time may lead to:

   d. All of the above

9. It's very unusual to experience unwanted memories after returning from the war zone.

   False

10. Anger is a "bad" emotion that can only lead to conflict and aggression.

    False

11. We all have dreams every night that we sleep.

    True

12. Antidepressants can mess up our sleep cycle.

    True

13. Taking a 60-minute nap can mess up the sleep cycle.

    True

14. If you cannot fall asleep at night, it is best to do something highly stressful to make you tired and help you fall asleep.

    False

15. Working all the time to try to avoid distressing war memories is a good way to deal with post-war stress.

    False

▶ PTSD symptom screens

The Primary Care PTSD Screen (PC-PTSD; Prins et al., 2004) is a valid and reliable screening measure for PTSD, and research continues to be conducted to determine its effectiveness with various populations. Those who evidence PTSD symptoms during the acute stage are more likely to develop the disorder. We recommend administering this screen to veterans before and after the intervention to measure improvement as well as to identify individuals who will need further assessment and/or treatment.

The PC-PTSD consists of four items. The screen includes an introductory sentence to cue respondents to traumatic events. The authors suggest that in most circumstances the results of the PC-PTSD should be considered "positive" if a patient answers "yes" to any three items. A cutoff score of two can be used to optimize sensitivity. Those screening positive should then receive a full assessment with a structured interview for PTSD.

▶ PC PTSD

Have you ever had an experience that was so frightening, horrible, or upsetting that, in the past month, you . . .

1. Have had nightmares about it or thought about it when you did not want to?

   Yes or No

2. Tried hard not to think about it or went out of your way to avoid situations that reminded you of it?

   Yes or No

3. Were constantly on guard, watchful, or easily startled?

   Yes or No

4. Felt numb or detached from others, activities, or your surroundings?

   Yes or No

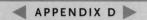

Chapter Quizzes Answer Key

▶ **Chapter 1—Understanding Transition Stress Reactions Quiz**

Leaders' Answer Key

1. What term refers to going out of our way *not* to think about or to keep away from something:

   a. Hypervigilance

   b. **Avoidance**

   c. Reexperiencing

   d. Dropping out

2. It's very unusual to experience unwanted memories after returning from the war zone.

   ■ **False:** Following combat or other highly stressful experiences, several types of reexperiencing symptoms are quite common—including intrusive thoughts, memories, dreams, and nightmares.

3. Although reminders of stressful combat events can feel overwhelming, the reaction to reminders often lessens with time.

   ■ **True:** Common initial reactions to highly stressful events, including combat, can feel quite overwhelming. However, in most cases, they lessen over time. If they persist, or are severe, it may be important to seek additional treatment.

4. Isolating from other people means loss of support, friendship, and closeness with others, and more time to worry or feel hopeless and alone.

   ■ **True:** Although the desire to isolate and avoid is a common reaction to combat stress, isolation can be very harmful in terms of reducing support and increasing opportunities for rumination and feelings of worry and loneliness.

5. What does SUDS stand for?

   a. Strong Underpinnings of Denial and Suppression

   b. **Subjective Units of Distress Scale**

c. The stuff you find floating at the top of beer

d. Soap scum Under Da Sink

6. Working all the time to try to avoid distressing memories of the stressful event is a good way to deal with post-war stress.

- **False:** As with other forms of avoidance, working all of the time typically serves to prolong the effects of transition stress. Thus, although staying active can be a helpful part of successful coping, using work (or anything else) as a means to avoid addressing transition stress results in fewer opportunities for positive experiences and feelings of achievement.

▶ Chapter 2—Stress Management Quiz

Leader's Answer Key

1. What are some common symptoms of long-term stress?
   a. Irritability
   b. Upset stomach, nausea, diarrhea
   c. Stiff neck or headaches
   d. **All of these are common**

2. Which of these are **positive ways** to cope with stress?
   a. **Exercise**
   b. Driving fast in your car
   c. Drinking a case of beer
   d. All of these are a positive way to cope with stress

3. Which of these are **negative ways** to cope with stress?
   a. Obsessing or worrying about things
   b. Smoking marijuana
   c. Road raging
   d. **All of these are not good**

4. What would be an example of a **mind-centered** stress management skill?
   a. Guided imagery
   b. Self-hypnosis
   c. Autogenics
   d. **All of these are mind-centered skills**

5. This is a relaxation skill where you breathe in with your belly coming out, and exhaling and your belly coming back in. It is very easy and helps people to relax. **What is it called?**
   a. Autoreflex breathing
   b. Deep muscle breathing
   c. **Diaphragmatic breathing**
   d. Exhalation Therapy

Leader's Answer Key

1. Reactive coping tools are behaviors that we use to prepare ourselves for problems that might occur in the future.

   - **False:** This is a description of proactive coping tools. Reactive coping tools are skills and behaviors that we do in response to a problem.

2. Social isolation helps protect a person from problems, and is a good way to help a person adjust to being back home after a deployment.

   - **False:** A person's mood and overall adjustment to being back from a deployment will be improved by social activities and resisting the urge to isolate. Social activities are healthy for the brain, and also provide more opportunities for positive experiences with others.

3. Setting and achieving goals is an important way to improve mood and decrease depression.

   - **True:** Even meeting small and moderate goals can help to produce a feeling of empowerment and mastery that helps to break the spiral of depression and start making positive changes.

4. When a person feels anxious in a situation that used to be comfortable, it means that they should get out of that situation as quickly as they can, and avoid that situation in the future.

   - **False:** Remember that after highly stressful events, the part of the brain called the amygdala sometimes becomes overactive and produces feelings of anxiety and fear even when nothing is going wrong. As a result, people may avoid doing things that were related to danger in a warzone, but that will not really lead to danger back home—such as being in crowds, going to movie theaters, or sitting with ones back to the door. However, it is important to help our brain and body learn the difference between what is dangerous and what is merely uncomfortable. The only way to do this is to practice being active again and give ourselves the chance to relearn that most activities are safe. This means *not* avoiding situations that may cause anxiety, but which are not actually dangerous.

5. As soon as we start doing pleasant activities, we should expect that our mood will change completely, and everything will be okay.

   - **False:** the positive spiral of activities that help reduce depression and elevate overall mood can be a slow process. It is important to remember that at first activities may not feel very good—this is part of feeling depressed. However, over time, with positive actions our mood improves, motivation increases, and even the activities themselves become more pleasurable.

6. When we experience very few activities we consider to be pleasant, we are more likely feel depressed. Also, when we feel depressed, we do not feel like doing the kinds of activities that are likely to be a source of pleasure. This is known as the:

   a. Complicated bereavement

   b. Sliding depressive cycle

c. **Downward spiral of depression**

d. Resilient coping

▶ Chapter 4—Sleep Quiz

Leader's Answer Key

1. We have dreams every night that we sleep.
   - **True:** Although most people do not remember their dreams, we all dream in cycles throughout the night

2. Sleeping in late is a good way to catch up on lost sleep.
   - **False:** Sleeping in late will interfere with the sleep cycle.

3. Alcohol and certain medications (such as Valium, Xanax, and over-the-counter sleep medications) can mess up our sleep cycle.
   - **True:** Although alcohol and certain sleep medications put us out, they work against our natural sleep cycle so that we do not feel restored after sleeping.

4. Antidepressants can mess up our sleep cycle.
   - **False:** Antidepressants (e.g., Wellbutrin, Lexapro, Prozac, Paxil) actually help restore our natural sleep cycle.

5. Taking a 60-minute nap can mess up the sleep cycle.
   - **True:** Taking naps longer than 30 minutes tends to interfere with the sleep cycle in the evening.

6. If you cannot fall asleep at night, it is best to perform a stressful, highly demanding task that will tire you out and help you fall asleep.
   - **False:** High demanding and stressful tasks will increase hormones like cortisol, which increase alertness and make it harder to fall asleep.

7. If you wake up and cannot get back to sleep, it is best to get out of bed (even in the middle of the night) and engage in a light, somewhat boring, activity.
   - **True:** It is best to perform a boring, nonstressful activity, such as reading a light novel, to prepare the body for sleep. Likewise, if you wake up at night and cannot get back to sleep, it is best to get out of bed (even in the middle of the night) and perform some nonstressful activity until you feel sleepy.

8. One way to cope with a nightmare is to write it down.
   - **True:** Writing down a nightmare makes the dream less real and helps you calm down faster. It can also be helpful to share the dream with someone close to you.

▶ Chapter 5—Dealing with Anger Quiz

Leader's Answer Key

1. Being angry for long period of time may lead to:
   a. High blood pressure
   b. Early death

c. Stomach disorders

d. **All of the above**

2. Which of the following is an **unhelpful** thing to do when you get very angry?

   a. Count to 10

   b. Take a time out

   c. **Try to argue your point**

   d. All of the above

3. Which of the following is a **helpful** use of your anger?

   a. Use anger to help you work harder

   b. Use anger to help motivate you to reach a goal

   c. Use anger to help you solve a problem

   d. **All of the above**

4. If your anger level is 5 or over (on a scale from 1 to 10) you should perform a healthy coping behavior.

   ■ **True:** When our anger goes above a 5, our thinking and our overall level of functioning is actually lowered. In addition to damage to our body from chronic anger, we are also more likely to act in foolish ways and get into more trouble. Using coping skills to reduce our anger when it begins to escalate helps us to manage situations better.

5. Returnees coming home from the war zone tend to be very calm and relaxed.

   ■ **False:** People returning from deployments often feel angry, on edge, and hyperalert. These are expected reactions that many people have following chronic stress in a combat zone, where anger may have often provided energy needed to survive life-threatening situations.

6. Anger is a "bad" emotion that can only lead to conflict and aggression.

   ■ **False:** Anger that is expressed in helpful ways can be very healthy. Channeled in a healthy way, anger can be used to give people energy, to help them reach their goals, and can motivate people to work harder, or help people to handle emergencies.

7. Name 3 cues that tell people when they are becoming angry:

   ■ Responses will vary, and may include a broad range of physiological and cognitive cues.

▶ **Chapter 6—Reintegrating with Society Quiz**

Leader's Answer Key

1. People who are hypervigilant:

   a. Always help other people who are in need

   b. Think they are sick even when they are well.

c. **Are overly alert for danger even when danger is not present.**

d. All of the above.

2. We can control every aspect of our environment and our life.

- **False:** There are many factors in life that are beyond our control. For example, one may not have control over where one is stationed, when and for how long one is deployed, other people's behavior in general, crowds, the weather, etc. After a deployment, other things may have changed as well, including the possibility of such things as not being in control of when memories of stressful events occur.

3. "Thinking" ahead is an important part of making healthy decisions and reintegrating with society.

- **True:** There are several predictable problems that may occur—for example, difficulties with friends and family, antimilitary statements or other offensive and insensitive statements, etc. Anticipating these types of problems and problem solving in advance how one might handle these situations, can help to head off numerous problems before they begin.

4. What are some situations or people that trigger stress reactions for you?

- **Responses will vary.**

5. What healthy coping behaviors can I use to deal with the people and/or situations that trigger stress reactions?

    Examples include:

- Communication skills

- Time-outs

- Other coping behaviors from earlier chapters

▶ **Chapter 7—Reintegrating with Family and Friends Quiz**

Leader's Answer Key

1. Veterans should be able to adjust back to family life easily and immediately after returning from the war zone.

- **False:** Given that both veterans and their families undergo changes during a deployment, it is natural for both to take time to readjust to being back together again.

2. Which of the following statements is an example of fighting fair?

a. **I feel angry when you tell me not to watch TV because I need time to relax.**

b. You always nag me when I watch TV.

c. You would not bother me if you loved me.

d. I feel like you are always nagging me.

3. Which of the following is a common change veterans may experience that may make it more difficult to reintegrate with the family:

   a. Loss of interest in activities that used to be enjoyable

   b. Difficulty trusting and feeling close to others

   c. Feeling a need to be in control at all times

   d. Not showing emotions besides anger

   e. Reluctant to talk about what happened in the war zone

   f. **All of the above**

4. Name 3 particular problems that frequently make reuniting as a couple, or with children, more difficult after deployment.

   Examples include:

   - Face to face communication may be hard at first.

   - Sexual closeness may also be awkward at first.

   - Losing interest in sexual activities, which may lead to your spouse or partner feeling hurt.

   - You may feel closer to your friends, and feel like your spouse or partner is a stranger.

   - Roles for basic household chores may have changed.

   - Spouses or partners may have become more independent and learned new coping skills.

   - You may have changed in your outlook and priorities in life.

   - Children have grown and may be different in many ways.

   - Your children may not recognize you, or may be slow to hug you.

   - Children may be very clingy, act younger than they are, or act indifferent, as if they do not care.

5. Name 4 things that may help with the transition back to being with family and friends (for example, making individual time to spend with each child or important family member).

   Examples include:

   - Taking time to listen to your spouse or partner, children, and other important family members.

   - Making individual time for each child and other important family members.

   - Taking time, such as a whole day away, for just you and your spouse or partner to renew your relationship.

   - Going slowly when reestablishing your place in the family.

   - Making efforts to explain to your family what you are feeling and what you would like.

   - Sharing with your family some stories about your deployment.

   - Supporting good things your family has done while you were gone.

   - Being prepared to make some adjustments.

Leader's Answer Key

1. List four positive things that you learned about yourself when you were deployed? (e.g., courage, ability to protect yourself, discipline).

   ■ Responses will vary.

2. What do you want your life to look like five years from now? Name four goals you have for yourself.

   ■ Responses will vary.

3. In this chapter, you identified some of your values, and ways a person who has those values might behave. Name some things you can do in the weeks and months ahead that are consistent with your values?

   ■ Responses will vary.

◀ **APPENDIX E** ▶

Stress Management Handouts

▶ **Identifying Stress Cues Worksheet**

A very important part of monitoring our stress is to identify how we react to things that happen in our lives. These are what we call "cues" because, if we pay attention to them, we will be able to know that we are in a high-stress situation. Please fill out each cue so that you can become more aware of what sets you off and stresses you out.

1. Physical cues (how your body responds to stress; e.g., increased heart rate, tightness in chest, upset stomach, feeling hot)

_____

_____

_____

2. Behavioral cues (what your body does; e.g., raised voice, clenched teeth/fist, pacing)

_____

_____

_____

3. Emotional cues (feelings that come up; e.g., fear, anger, sadness, guilt)

_____

_____

_____

4. Cognitive (thinking) cues (what we think about in response to the event; e.g., negative self-talk such as "I'm going to lose control," "I've got to get out of here," "I can't handle this")

_____

_____

_____

_____

▶ Identifying Stressful Events Worksheet

To manage your stress well, it is really important that you pay attention to and identify situations that make you feel anxious, nervous, or angry. Most of us are aware that there are certain "hot situations" we avoid because they make us feel uncomfortable.

The purpose of this worksheet is to help you define those "hot situations" *for you,* and how to identify when your anxiety or anger is being provoked. Sometimes these situations remind us of things that have happened in the past where we felt particularly anxious or angry.

1. What events or situations in the past have triggered a stress reaction in you?

   _____

   _____

   _____

2. What "hot situations" currently trigger a stress reaction in you?

   _____

   _____

   _____

▶ Weekly Stress Monitoring Worksheet

Use this sheet to record your stress during the week. You can still use this sheet in session to discuss what occurred that caused your stress to rise and what you did to manage the stress reaction. This can also be used to help you develop additional strategies to deal with similar situations in the future.

1. What was the highest number you reached on the Stress Meter during the past week?

   _____

   _____

   _____

2. What was the event that triggered your stress?

   _____

   _____

   _____

3. What cues were associated with the stress-inducing event?

    a. Physical Cues

    b. Behavioral Cues

    c. Emotional Cues

    d. Cognitive Cues

4. What strategies did you use to prevent hitting a 10 on the Stress Meter (assuming you did not hit a 10)?

    _____

    _____

    _____

5. For each day this week, monitor and record the highest number you reach on the Stress Meter.

    _____ Monday

    _____ Tuesday

    _____ Wednesday

    _____ Thursday

    _____ Friday

    _____ Saturday

    _____ Sunday

▶ Monitoring Stress and SUDS

Monitoring stress level is much like checking a temperature gauge on the wall inside your home. In order to effectively cope with your stress it is important to be aware of how stressed you are feeling. The gauge that we use to monitor stress or distress level is the subjective units of distress scale (SUDS).

What is your SUDS level right now, on a scale of 1 to 10—with 1 being very low stress and 10 being that you are so uncomfortable that you can hardly stand it?

Please refer to the SUDS below at this time. This will be the way that stress or distress level will be monitored or checked from time to time.

Completely Calm   Nervous Wreck

0   1   2   3   4   5   6   7   8   9   10

Clinician Follow-Up Questionnaire

We would like your feedback! If you care to provide your comments about this guide and workbook, please provide the following information. Send this form to:

Julia M. Whealin, Ph.D.
Deputy Director for Education/Research Health Scientist
3375 Koapaka Street, Suite I-560
Honolulu, HI 96819

Name (optional): _____

Profession/degree: _____

Organization (optional): _____

Clinic (optional): _____

City/State (optional): _____

Number of clients who used the workbook: _____

Dates of intervention: _____

Modalities used (individual, small group, classroom): _____

Client population: _____

▶ Overall Feedback

Ratings: 5 = Excellent   4 = Very Good   3 = Good   2 = Fair   1 = Poor

After completing this intervention, please evaluate each factor below according to the above scale.

		5	4	3	2	1	
Overall content (subject matter)		5	4	3	2	1	
Chapter quizzes		5	4	3	2	1	
Exercises		5	4	3	2	1	
Relevance to population		5	4	3	2	1	
Clients ability to implement intervention		5	4	3	2	1	
Difficulty level	(too hard)	1	2	3	2	1	(too easy)
Detail	(too detailed)	1	2	3	2	1	(too vague)
Length	(too long)	1	2	3	2	1	(too short)
Effectiveness of intervention		5	4	3	2	1	
Overall rating		5	4	3	2	1	

After completing this intervention, please provide feedback below.

What was most difficult about using this workbook/manual?

_____

_____

_____

What did you find most helpful when using this workbook/manual?

_____

_____

_____

Were there any problems that returnees encountered that made it difficult to implement the protocol?

_____

_____

_____

Was there a particular type of returnee who this workbook/intervention was not helpful with?

_____

_____

_____

Was there a particular type of returnee who this workbook/intervention was particularly helpful with?

_____

_____

_____

Did clients report improvements due to this intervention?

_____

_____

_____

Please offer any additional comments or improvements that you think might be helpful. Thank you for your feedback!

References

Alvarez, E., & Pitch, A. S. (2005). *Chained eagle: The heroic story of the first American shot down over North Vietnam.* Washington, DC: Potomac Books.

Alvarez, E., & Schreiner, S. A. (1991). *Code of conduct.* New York: D. I. Fine

Beck, A. T. (1988). *Love is never enough.* New York: Harper & Row.

Beck, A. T., Rush, A. J., Shaw, B. F., & Emery, G. (1979). *Cognitive therapy of depression.* New York: Guilford Press.

Beck, J. S. (1995). *Cognitive therapy: Basics and beyond.* New York: Guilford Press.

Bower, G. (1981). Mood and memory. *American Psychologist, 36,* 129–148.

Davis, J. L., & Wright, D. C. (2007). Randomized clinical trial for treatment of chronic nightmares in trauma-exposed adults. *Journal of Traumatic Stress, 20*(2), 123–133.

Dimidjian, S., Dobson, K. S., Kohlenberg, R. J., Gallop, R., Markleey, D. K., Atkins, D. C., et al. (2006). Randomized trial of behavioral activation, cognitive therapy, and antidepressant medication in the acute treatment of adults with major depression. *Journal of Consulting and Clinical Psychology, 74,* 658–670.

Drescher, K. D., Rosen, C. S., Burling, T. A., & Foy, D. W. (2003). Causes of death among male veterans who received residential treatment for PTSD. *Journal of Traumatic Stress, 16*(6), 535–543.

Edinger, J. D., Wohlgemuth, W. K., Radtke, R. A., Marsh, G. R., & Quillian, R. E. (2001). Cognitive-behavioral therapy for treatment of chronic primary insomnia. *Journal of the American Medical Association, 285,* 1856–1864.

Edleson, J. L., & Tolman, R. M. (1992). *Interventions for men who batter: An ecological approach.* Newbury Park, CA: Sage.

Follette, V. M., Ruzek, J. I., & Abueg, F. R (Eds). (1988). *Cognitive-behavioral therapies for trauma.* New York: Guilford Press.

Forbes, D., Phelps, A., & McHugh, T. (2001). Treatment of combat-related nightmares using imagery rehearsal: A pilot study. *Journal of Traumatic Stress, 14,* 433–442.

Gottman, J. M., & Silver, N. (1999). *The seven principles for making marriage work.* New York: Three Rivers Press.

Gray, J. A. (1988). *The psychology of fear and stress* (2nd ed.). Cambridge: Cambridge University Press.

Green, B. L. (2003). Traumatic stress and its consequences. In B. L. Green, M. Friedman, J. de Jong, S. Solomon, T. Keane, J. Fairbank, et al. (Eds.), *Trauma interventions in war and peace: Prevention, practice, and policy* (pp. 17–32). New York: Kluwer Academic/Plenum Press.

Guerney, B. (1977). *Relationship enhancement.* San Francisco: Jossey-Bass.

Hopko, D. R., Lejuez, C. W., Ruggiero, K. J., & Eifert, G. H. (2003). Contemporary behavioral activation treatments for depression: Procedures, principles, and progress. *Clinical Psychology Review, 23,* 699–717.

Jacobs, G. D. (1998). *Say good night to insomnia.* New York: Henry Holt.

Jacobson, N. S., & Christensen, A. (1996). *Acceptance and change in couple therapy: A therapist's guide to transforming relationships.* New York: Norton.

Klein, R. H., & Schermer, V. L. (Eds). (2000). *Group psychotherapy for psychological trauma.* New York: Guilford Press.

Krakow, B., Johnston, L., Melendrez, D., Hollifield, M., Warner, T. D., Chavez-Kennedy, D., et al. (2001). An open-label trial of evidence-based cognitive behavior therapy for nightmares and insomnia in crime victims with PTSD. *American Journal of Psychiatry, 158,* 2043–2047.

Krystal, A. D., & Davidson, J. R. T. (2007). The use of Prazosin for the treatment of trauma nightmares and sleep disturbance in combat veterans with post-traumatic stress disorder. *Biological Psychiatry, 61*(8), 925–927

Kubany, E. S. (1998). Cognitive therapy for trauma-related guilt. In V. M. Follette, J. I. Ruzek, & F. R. Abueg (Eds.), *Cognitive-behavioral therapies for trauma* (pp. 124–161). New York: Guilford Press.

LeDoux, J. (2002). *Synaptic self: How our brains become who we are.* New York: Penguin.

Lewinsohn, P. M., Hoberman, H., Teri, L., & Hautziner, M. (1985). An integrative theory of depression. In S. Reiss & R. Bootzine (Eds.), *Theoretical issues in behavior therapy* (p. 176). New York: Academic Press.

Library of Congress. (2007). Video interview with John S. McCain, III. In *Stories from the Veterans History Project.* Retrieved Sepember 24, 2007, from http://lcweb2.loc.gov/diglib/vhp-stories/loc.natlib.afc2001001.07736/.

Litz, B. T. (2004). Closing remarks. In B.T. Litz (Ed.), *Early intervention for trauma and traumatic loss* (pp. 319–326). New York: Guilford Press.

Meichenbaum, D. H. (1985). *Stress inoculation training.* New York: Pergamon Press.

Meichenbaum, D. H., & Deffenbacher, J. L. (1988). Stress inoculation training. *Counseling Psychologist, 16,* 69–90.

Murtagh, D. R., & Greenwood, K. M. (1995). Identifying effective psychological treatments for insomnia: A meta-analysis. *Journal of Consulting and Clinical Psychology, 63,* 79–89.

Norris, F. H., & Hamblen, J. L. (2004). Standardized self-report measures of civilian trauma and PTSD. In J. P. Wilson, T. M. Keane, & T. Martin (Eds.), *Assessing psychological trauma and PTSD* (pp. 63–102). New York: Guilford Press.

Paymar, M. (1993). *Violent no more: Helping men end domestic abuse.* Alameda, CA: Hunter House.

Pence, E., & Paymar, M. (1993). *Education groups for men who batter: The Duluth Model.* New York: Springer.

Prins, A., Ouimette, P., Kimerling, R., Camerond, R. P., Hugelshofer, D. S., Shaw-Hegwer, J., et al. (2004). The primary care PTSD screen (PC-PTSD): Development and operating characteristics. *Primary Care Psychiatry, 9*(1), 9–14.

Raphael, B., & Wooding, S. (2004). Early mental health intervention for traumatic loss in adults. In B. T. Litz (Ed.), *Early intervention for trauma and traumatic loss* (pp. 147–178). New York: Guilford Press.

Ready, D. J., Brown-Thomas, K. R., Worley, V., Backscheider, A. G., Harvey, L. C., Baltzell, D., et al. (in press). A field test of group based exposure therapy with 102 veterans with war-related posttraumatic stress disorder. *Journal of Traumatic Stress.*

Reilly, P. M., & Shopshire, M. S. (2002). *Anger management for substance abuse and mental health clients: A cognitive behavioral therapy manual* (DHHS Publication No. SMA 02-3661). Rockville, MD: Center for Substance Abuse Treatment, Substance Abuse and Mental Health Services Administration.

Resick, P. A., & Schnicke, M. K. (1993). *Cognitive processing therapy for rape victims: A treatment manual.* Newbury Park, CA: Sage.

Rosenbaum, A., & Leisring, P. A. (2001). Group intervention programs for batterers. In R. A. Geffner & A. Rosenbaum (Eds.), *Domestic violence offenders: Current interventions, research, and implications for policies and standards* (pp. 57–72). New York: Haworth Press.

Rothbaum, B. O., Foa, E. B., Riggs, D. S., Murdock, T., & Walsh, W. (1992). A prospective examination of posttraumatic stress disorder in rape victims. *Journal of Traumatic Stress, 5,* 455–475.

Saxon, A. J., Davis, T. M., Sloan, K. L., McKnight, K. M., McFall, M. E., & Kivlahan, D. R. (2001). Trauma, symptoms of posttraumatic stress disorder, and associated problems among incarcerated veterans. *Psychiatric Services, 52*(7), 959–964.

Seligman, M. E. (1991). Power and powerlessness: Comments on "cognates of personal control." *Applied and Preventive Psychology, 1,* 119–120.

Snyder, M. (1981). Seek, and ye shall find: Testing hypotheses about other people. In E. Higgins, C. Herman, & M. Zannz (Eds.), *Social cognition: The Ontario Symposium.* Hillsdale, NJ: Erlbaum.

Uricchio, M. (2001, July 9). Breakfast with . . . Everett Alvarez Jr. *Pittsburgh Post Gazette.*

Wolpe, J. (1973). *The practice of behavior therapy* (2nd ed.). New York: Pergamon Press.

Weathers, F., Litz, B., Herman, D., Huska, J., & Keane, T. (1993, October). *The PTSD Checklist (PCL): Reliability, Validity, and Diagnostic Utility.* Paper presented at the Annual Convention of the International Society for Traumatic Stress Studies, San Antonio, TX.

Index